Praise for *Stop Spoiling That Man*

"Dr. Arden's book goes beyo   g;
it tells you precisely what *you*   ay
relationship."

—**ALBERT J. BERNSTEIN**, author, *Emotional Vampires*

"If you have ever wanted to make your man a better man, this is your guidebook. It is a practical, concrete, and thorough guide with easy-to-remember names. It is like Dr. and Mrs. Arden are sitting there right next to you, asking all the right questions, and getting you to see for yourself what needs to be done. It has ingenious, yet simple ways, of dealing with difficult situations in relationships."

—**DR. JAY CARTER**, author, *Nasty People*

"Relationships can be very confusing. When things don't go right, you can't tell if it's your fault or his. In *Stop Spoiling That Man*, psychologist John Arden brings his many years of experience helping couples understand who's doing what to whom. In this easy-to-read book, Dr. Arden clarifies the dynamics of dependency in romantic relationships and gives practical advice on how to set limits on needy behavior. This book can help make your relationship much less confusing. A good read!"

—**SCOTT WETZLER, PHD**, author,
Living With the Passive-Aggressive Man

Praise for *Stop Spoiling That Man*

"Are you sick and tired of dealing with immature, demanding, or needy men? Buy this book! It's packed with innovative, pragmatic ways to speak up and stand up for yourself so men (or anyone) can no longer take advantage of your good nature. Read it and reap."
—SAM HORN, author, *Tongue Fu!* and *What's Holding You Back?*

"*Stop Spoiling That Man* could only be written by a man—because it takes one to know one! Dr. John Arden (with great sidebars by his wife) helps women identify the subtle and not-so-subtle ways that some men act entitled and get women to conform to their needs. Most importantly, the book empowers women to make a clear and assertive stand and bring out the best qualities in themselves and their partners."
—DAVID B. WEXLER, PhD, author, *When Good Men Behave Badly: Change Your Behavior, Change Your Relationship*, and executive director, Relationship Training Institute (San Diego)

"In *Stop Spoiling That Man*, Dr. Arden takes a look at the shadow side of the modern marriage. The over-functioning and often resentful female can contribute greatly to the spoiling of her partner. The spoiled man looks back at her and asks, 'why are you so stressed out?' From this, a lack of passion ensues that can turn the best romance into a rotten apple. Dr. Arden walks us through this gently and with a sense of humor. The ultimate goal is to reinvigorate the male/female partnership. I will certainly recommend this book to members of my relationship group!"
—JOANNA MANQUEROS, LCSW

Praise for *Stop Spoiling That Man*

"Dr. Arden has presented the concept of spoiling in a gentle, nonblaming, nonjudgmental manner. Indeed, his method is empowering, supportive, and encouraging to women who want to maintain their relationships in a dignified way with a real action-oriented, coherent plan. This is a must-read guide written in user-friendly terms for women (and men) who want to refresh and preserve their relationship."

—STEVE MILLER, LCSW

"Many women will be encouraged by this unique self-help book. They will find vivid examples of familiar relationship stalemates, along with suggestions on how to break the pattern without breaking up the relationship. This book will help the partners of 'spoiled men' regain their sense of self and avoid the pitfalls of the same old arguments. I believe the book carries through on its promise to raise the level of communication between spouses to a higher level. I wish I had had this book to recommend to the many women who participated in my boundary-building groups for women. I look forward to its publication so that I can recommend it in the future."

—JIANNE GIMIAN, PhD

STOP
Spoiling
THAT MAN

Turn Your Needy Guy into
an Equal, *Loving Partner*

John B. Arden, Ph.D., with Victoria Arden, M.A.

Adams**media**

Avon, Massachusetts

Published by
Adams Media, an F+W Publications Company
57 Littlefield Street
Avon, MA 02322
www.adamsmedia.com

ISBN-10: 1-59869-328-X
ISBN-13: 978-1-59869-328-7

Printed in the United States of America.

J I H G F E D C B A

Library of Congress Cataloging-in-Publication Data
is available from the publisher.

This publication is designed to provide accurate and authoritative information with regard to the subject matter covered. It is sold with the understanding that the publisher is not engaged in rendering legal, accounting, or other
professional advice. If legal advice or other expert assistance is required, the
services of a competent professional person should be sought.
—From a *Declaration of Principles* jointly adopted by a Committee of the
American Bar Association and a Committee of Publishers and Associations

Many of the designations used by manufacturers and sellers to distinguish
their product are claimed as trademarks. Where those designations appear
in this book and Adams Media was aware of a trademark claim, the designations have been printed with initial capital letters.

This book is available at quantity discounts for bulk purchases.
For information, please call 1-800-289-0963.

My appreciation goes to my agent Ed Knappman for finding a good home for this book at Adams. And to Katrina Schroeder, Jennifer Kushnier, and Laura Daly, who applied their exceptional editorial skills to craft this book to be far better than what it was when they received it. I am also grateful to my wife, Vicki, for participating in the development of this book. She has provided useful and clarifying sidebars throughout each chapter. She is my best friend and life partner. Her perspective has always helped me grow. I also want to thank our sons, Paul and Gabe. Most parents cherish their children and believe that they are beyond stellar. I am no exception. They have already gone far beyond my accomplishments when I was their ages. I am proud of them. As my late father would say often, Vicki is the best mother both boys could ever have asked for.

CONTENTS

Introduction

Because you picked up this book, you may be like millions of other women who seek help dealing with their relationships. Specifically, these women complain that their husbands or boyfriends demand too much and give back too little—that their men are spoiled. Unfortunately, what you may not realize is that you, like so many other women, may be the one doing the spoiling or, at the very least, rewarding the very behavior you complain about. Like so many women, you may have thought at one time or another that your husband or boyfriend is spoiled, and silently (or openly) cursed his mother for spoiling him. Even if his mother was the one who started spoiling him, you may be continuing where she left off. In order to save your relationship, you'll need to learn what is truly spoiled behavior and what is not. If he is indeed spoiled, you'll also need to learn how not to continue where his mother left off.

Fortunately, I have led a relationship group (attended mostly by women) for fifteen years and have worked with hundreds of women like you. In the process, I've taught them how they can successfully unspoil their men and build better relationships. I present that information here.

This book will provide you with practical and easy ways to identify and understand spoiled men; more importantly, it will help you learn how to deal with them. Each chapter describes personalities and behavior of spoiled men, offers practical suggestions for handling them, and illustrates conflicts with vignettes using composites of individuals and couples I've worked with. I've included mnemonics I created in my therapy groups to help you remember how to remain focused on relationship-enhancing and self-protecting skills.

The book will also explain how to distinguish a truly spoiled man from one who really isn't. It dissects the various ways that spoiled men control women and offers a wide range of methods to deal with such men. In other words, it offers a solution to the problem by giving you the psychological tools you need to use to transform him into an equal partner.

Before we move on to what this book will offer you, I want to point out that if your relationship is "over the line" and includes alcoholism, domestic violence, or verbal abuse, you will need to address those issues immediately before this book can help.

Carrying on a relationship with someone who is abusing alcohol is a losing proposition. If your husband or boyfriend abuses alcohol or drugs, we can say that his brain is toxic. You will not be able to change his behavior if he has a toxic brain. You will need to get help with your codependency. There are many great self-help community groups that you can attend such as Al-Anon and CoDA meetings. If you belong to a large HMO, there are support groups that can help you find your way through the difficult waters of a relationship marred by substance abuse. A national substance-abuse facility locator can be found at this Web site: *http://dasis3.samhsa.gov*. Follow the links to locate a program in your area. Once you have located a program, ask for family or codependency programs in your area.

If your relationship is traumatized by domestic violence, you need help immediately to keep safe. As a society we have moved far ahead of where we were twenty years ago, thanks to changes in the legal system and sensational legal trials such as the O.J. Simpson case. Almost every county provides domestic violence programs including safe houses and legal support. In the past I was a member of the Board of Directors of one such program that provided a full range of services, so I can tell you first-hand that help is out there. The bottom line is that this book is simply not for you now if your relationship includes domestic violence. Get safe! Call this number for help: 1-800- 799-SAFE (7233) or go to this Web site: *www.ndvh.org.*

If your relationship is marred by verbal abuse, you must deal with that before moving on to this book. Of course, there is a matter of degree. Where do you draw the line? To be practical, let's say that if your relationship is filled with frequent demeaning putdowns in which he swears at you and tells you that you are worth nothing outside of your relationship with him, he is way over the line. There are many good books and support groups out there. One good book is entitled *The Verbally Abusive Relationship* by Patricia Evans. I would also demand that he attend an anger management group as a condition for you to remain in the relationship.

Now, if your relationship is not way over the line, let's move on to what this book can offer you.

Part I of the book will help you identify the main characteristics of spoiled men and the things you do to spoil them. It will also describe the main characteristics of a healthy relationship and how a spoiled man can challenge you to forget about them.

It's surprisingly easy to drift into a lopsided relationship with a man who consumes rather than shares and who takes rather than gives. Chapter 1 describes the different types of spoiled men and various techniques they use to get you to spoil them. In Chapter 2 you'll learn the principles associated with healthy relationships. If a man is spoiled, he probably doesn't follow these principles. You'll learn to stay focused on the healthy principles while deflecting his efforts to get you to spoil him.

From the beginning of a relationship, you need to be alert to red flags that signal a spoiled man. When feelings well up in you in response to his spoiled behavior, they wear down your sense of self. If you don't respond to these red flags, you find yourself in emotional quicksand where those feelings get overwhelming. You'll learn how to deal with the red flags in Chapter 3.

WHEN OUR PUBLISHER asked for a woman's perspective in this book, I was happy to accept. So, who am I? I'm an educator, I've worked in mental health, I'm a mother, and I happen to be married to the author. My aim is to provide sidebars that contain an informational nugget that should stick in your memory.

In Part II you'll learn the various roles that a spoiled man can use to get you to go easy on him. A spoiled man can play the victim role with such expertise that he demands sympathy and elicits guilt. He encourages you to assume that you are his victimizer. You'll learn how to escape and deflect this unwarranted blame in Chapter 4, how to detach from his emotional storm and let him stew in his own self-pity in Chapter 5, how to remain optimistic about your own life while not being brought down by his pessimism in Chapter 6, how to communicate on a level high above the eggshells he sprinkles around himself in Chapter 7, how to remain appropriately sympathetic to a hypochondriac without becoming an enabler in Chapter 8, and how to avoid communicating on his level while at the same time inviting him to communicate on your level in Chapter 9.

Part III classifies different types of spoiled men and describes how you can avoid spoiling them. Passive Pete can manipulate you into spoiling him by his passivity; you'll learn how to demand more from him while bypassing his defensiveness in Chapter 10. Slippery Sam is fast and loose with the facts and an expert at sweet-talking you; you'll learn how to hold him accountable and keep him on his toes wondering if you know the truth about what he's doing and saying in Chapter 11.

Magnificent Mike tries to convince you that you should be there for him more than he needs to be there for you; you'll learn to pull the covers off his ploys and turn a one-way street into a two-way street in Chapter 12. Traditional Tom hides behind tradition or even his "pious" interpretation of a religious text to get you to cater to him, but he fails to reciprocate; you'll learn a variety of ways to bring him into the twenty-first century and avoid spoiling him in Chapter 13. At the end of each section you'll find a little quiz. It is meant to bring home the points that I raise in each chapter.

Now let's get on to how to identify a spoiled man. Once you learn to identify him, we can move on to how he challenges a healthy relationship and what to look out for so that you can prevent spoiling him.

PART ONE

breaking down
the characteristics
of *spoiled* men

1
Identifying Spoiled Men

Is the man in your life spoiled? You're probably reading this because you think so. If he is, don't worry! There is still hope to transform him into an equal partner. But first, you must determine whether or not he *is* spoiled. Answer yes or no to the following questions:

1. Do his problems come first and yours third, behind the dog's?
   ○ Yes   ○ No

2. Does he complain about everything from an itchy toe to a cloudy day?
   ○ Yes   ○ No

3. Does he have an excuse for everything?
   ○ Yes   ○ No

4. When you do projects together, does he stand back and watch you do all the work?
   ○ Yes   ○ No

5. When you have a headache, does he tell you he has a migraine?
   ○ Yes ○ No

6. When he's in a bad mood, does it feel like a weather front just blew in?
   ○ Yes ○ No

7. Does he make you feel like you're walking on eggshells?
   ○ Yes ○ No

8. Do his eyes glaze over as he pretends to listen to you?
   ○ Yes ○ No

9. Does he criticize decisions you've made, even though he refused to participate in making them?
   ○ Yes ○ No

10. Does he use emotional blackmail, such as getting grumpy, to get what he wants?
    ○ Yes ○ No

11. Does he try to make you feel guilty for not giving him more even though you've given him too much?
    ○ Yes ○ No

12. Does he put you in a position of acting like his mother?
    ○ Yes ○ No

To how many of these questions did you answer yes? The main principle here is that he acts spoiled when he demands more from you than is healthy for you to give. The more yes answers, the more spoiled he is—and at your own expense. The question is: Are you going to spoil him? It takes two to spoil:

he can't be spoiled unless someone spoils him. Ask yourself the following questions:

1. Do you feel like you need to boost him up all the time?
   ○ Yes ○ No

2. Are you always cleaning up after him?
   ○ Yes ○ No

3. Do you feel guilty if you don't give him what he wants?
   ○ Yes ○ No

4. Does he always get his way because you don't want to disappoint him?
   ○ Yes ○ No

5. Do you take the blame for something he did?
   ○ Yes ○ No

6. Do you make excuses for him to family and friends?
   ○ Yes ○ No

7. Do you feel like you can't do enough to make him happy?
   ○ Yes ○ No

8. Do you put his needs ahead of yours?
   ○ Yes ○ No

9. Do you mother him just like his own mother?
   ○ Yes ○ No

10. Do you always make decisions for both of you when he passively sits on the sidelines?
    ○ Yes ○ No

Count up your score. If you answered yes to more than two of these questions, you're sending him a powerful message. Though you aren't literally saying it, you're making it clear that you aim to spoil him.

You may have asked yourself: "Is it me? Am I not trying hard enough? Or is it him?" The answer is: It's both of you. He may trick you into spoiling him, but you take his bait.

You may protest: "Wouldn't he see that I love him and try harder to meet me halfway?" Not necessarily. If you always go more than halfway, he doesn't need to meet you there. He can sit back and let you make the effort. Some men simply can't refuse your extra effort, and they'll stay spoiled. This book will help you invite him to meet you as an equal partner.

The following story of Mara and Kyle will give you a taste of how a spoiled man can test out a woman to see how far he can pull her into spoiling him. Notice how she initially felt compassion and concern for him during a time of need.

MARA AND KYLE

Mara came in for counseling after the third month of dating Kyle. Their relationship had been going along for about two months without any obvious flaws, except that Kyle seemed to have suffered a string of unfortunate losses. In addition to having suffered frequent back pain, his car was repossessed, and he lost his best friend.

Mara told me that she felt terrible for Kyle. She tried to make sure that he got as much support as she could provide and wanted my input to help her balance the demands of her busy life while being there for him. She gave him money to make the payments for his new car and brought groceries every time she came over to visit. Usually she'd put away the groceries herself because Kyle was on the couch looking like he was suffering from back pain.

She began to feel taken for granted after he stopped thanking her. It seemed to her that he expected her to bring food. But she wasn't ready to say anything about these feelings. She worried that if she said something critical about their relationship he'd feel hurt during a time of need. Already she felt like she was walking on eggshells. So she stuck it out and said nothing.

She called him often to check in because she knew he expected it. He called too but the conversations were troubling for her. For example, he called often during her busy afternoons at work. One day, after her first counseling session, she thought about letting the call ring over to voice mail. As it rang she worried that her boss was trying to reach her about the upcoming audit by the state reviewers, so she answered it.

"Hi, it's me," Kyle said in a tone that seemed to drop off into moroseness.

"Oh, hi! How are you feeling?"

"Not good."

"What's the problem?"

"You name it. Where do I start?"

Mara glanced nervously at the inventory list that she had promised to have done an hour ago. "Listen, how 'bout I come by later? My boss is . . ."

"It's my back, and now my sinuses. You know that Christmas tree, it's shedding needles all over. . . ."

"Kyle," Mara cut in, knowing that she had bought the tree. "I've gotta go. I'll be by tonight."

"What? Now you don't have time for me?"

"Yes, yes, I do, but . . ."

"That's better. Anyway, as I was saying . . ."

Later that evening Mara brought takeout food over for dinner. When she handed him the containers he sighed. "Oh, Chinese food," he said in a disappointed voice.

As she stared at the takeout containers feeling guilty, he went to lie down on the couch to watch television. She glanced at a pile of papers lying on the kitchen table. Curiosity got the best of her. She shuffled through the papers and found a letter from his employer. It began by pointing out that it was one of a series of similar letters that addressed his tendency to come in late and leave early.

Kyle walked in. At first she flinched, worried that he would think she was being nosy. Then she realized that he saw her holding the paper. She decided that she might as well go with whatever he threw her way.

"So now you're reading my mail?" he said.

"I was trying to clear off a place for dinner," she said. "Why would your employer write to you?"

"Those jerks think they're going to get away with that!"

Mara glanced down at the letter and pretended to read it while she tried to think of what to say. "You're so undeserving of this. They've got no right to be critical of you. You've always said that everyone loves you there and can't get along without you. Right?"

"Sure," he responded unconvincingly. "Uh . . . Anyway, maybe you could throw something together for dinner? I'm not wild about Chinese food."

She realized it was time to start letting him know that she would no longer spoil him or put his supposed needs in front of her own. "Maybe you can make something for yourself," she said, gathering her things. "I'll take the Chinese food home. I've got to get up early tomorrow for work."

This story illustrates how even in the early dating part of a relationship a man can test you to see how willing you are to spoil him. In the beginning, Mara responded to what she thought was a legitimate need for support. Eventually it became clear that his neediness far exceeded what was healthy for their relationship. This was the first step in showing that she would not take care of him beyond what was reasonable. Through counseling she was able to make it clear to Kyle that she would not spoil him and that she offered only a healthy, mutually giving relationship.

> PLAIN AND SIMPLE, a spoiled man is needy. He'll manipulate you with tactics that sometimes are overt and sometimes are subtle forms of neediness. Don't confuse his being needy with a legitimate need for your support.

BREAKDOWN OF SPOILED MEN

To learn how to avoid spoiling your man, first you'll need to learn the tricks that spoiled men use to get you to spoil them. While some spoiled men are blatantly obvious like Kyle, some are not. The obvious ones openly demand that you spoil them. Less obvious ones manipulate you into spoiling them by playing on your sympathy or sense of duty. I break down these spoiled men into four basic characters, which I cover in greater depth in Part III:

- **Passive Pete**: He uses passivity and playing the victim to get you to take care of him. Sometimes you feel like cuddling him and telling him that he'll be okay. It's not what he does, but what he doesn't do that gets you to spoil him. There are times you feel like you have to baby him because he pretends to be incapable of taking care of himself.
- **Slippery Sam**: Smooth and charming, he plays fast and loose with the facts. He overspends on himself, and you find out about it only by accident. He distorts the truth about himself but insists on knowing the truth from you.
- **Magnificent Mike**: He uses a pumped-up sense of being "special" to get you to meet his needs. He may have a special talent that you respect or he may be revered by others. He has no ability to laugh at himself. But in an

airplane he'll accept a first-class upgrade and see no problem leaving you in coach.

- **Traditional Tom:** He may hide behind tradition or a self-serving interpretation of a religious text to get you to wait on him. He says he's "old-fashioned." The truth is, he's stuck in the time warp of sexism and patriarchal control.

Granted, some spoiled men are composites of two or more of these types. But to better explain how spoiled men behave, I'll describe each type in more detail. You'll learn what each has in his bag of tricks and how to resist falling for those tricks. After reading this chapter, you can choose which chapter in Part III to follow up on later. Let's meet the guys:

Passive Pete

Consider Passive Pete. He uses passivity to get you to spoil him. One of his tricks is to be moody. Another is to play on your sense of guilt or sympathy. Or he may control you by the way he overdefends himself. But if he's like most Passive Petes, he uses a combination of all these methods.

I CALL PASSIVE PETE *Energy-Drain Man*. He's so entrenched in feeling low or feeling nothing that he needs others to provide the emotional uplift he needs to feel alive. He was probably drawn to you for your positive outlook. He may kindle your maternal instincts. But don't forget that you're not his mother!

He can suck the emotional energy out of you. Even though he doesn't say it, he wants you to baby him emotionally. He pulls you into taking care of him by:

- Controlling the emotional climate of the household
- Being indecisive and passively encouraging you to make decisions for both of you

- Encouraging you to feel guilty for having made decisions that turned out badly
- Making little effort to meet you halfway in conversation, then saying that you talk too much
- Acting needy and implying that it is because of low self-esteem
- Being grumpy and always having a good excuse why he is
- Encouraging you to feel guilty when he's in a bad mood, as if you caused it
- Requiring you to cheer him up
- Being pessimistic and encouraging you get him to look on the bright side

If you give him what he wants, you can make things worse. In other words, by falling for his tricks, you'll spoil him even more. Ask yourself the following questions:

1. When he passively encourages you to make the decisions for both of you, do you do it?
   ◯ Yes ◯ No

2. When he complains about a decision you made that turns out imperfectly, do you feel guilty?
   ◯ Yes ◯ No

3. When he fails to meet you halfway in conversation, do you go well beyond halfway to compensate?
   ◯ Yes ◯ No

4. Do you pamper him when he's grumpy?
   ◯ Yes ◯ No

5. Are you always buying into his excuses for his moods?
   ◯ Yes ◯ No

6. Do you sometimes have to cancel events you've counted on because of his moods?
   ○ Yes   ○ No

7. Do you sometimes feel compelled to "find out what's wrong," even though you must drag clues out of him as if you were playing 20 Questions?
   ○ Yes   ○ No

8. Do you hold back from telling him about your feelings?
   ○ Yes   ○ No

9. Do you worry that you might say something that will get him in a bad mood?
   ○ Yes   ○ No

10. When he gives you the silent treatment for something he said you did, are you the one who has to break the ice?
    ○ Yes   ○ No

If you answered any of the above questions with a yes, you're inviting him to be spoiled. You'll need to protect yourself from his efforts to suck you into spoiling him. I'm not saying that you should be cold. But I am saying that you shouldn't do for him what he can do for himself.

Passive Pete is like a vacuum. You get sucked in by feeling responsible for him, feeling guilty if you don't take care of him, and feeling sorry for him. For a detailed description of Passive Pete and the type of tricks he uses, turn to Chapter 10. There I'll explain how you can invite him to be your equal partner.

Slippery Sam

Let's turn to Slippery Sam. You know how difficult it is to hold a wet bar of soap. When you try to grab it off the shower floor, it slips out of your hand again. That's like dealing with Slippery Sam. When you think you've pinned him down to hold him accountable for something, he's got a good story for you. You're left scratching your head wondering what happened.

Slippery Sam is fast and loose with the facts. He twists, distorts, and hides the truth. Because he damages the truth, you're put into a position of looking for verification that what he says is true. He might tell you that he already took out the trash if you ask him to do it. When you go to check the can, it's still full. Then when you point that out, he says, "Oh, I thought you meant did I do it yesterday."

He may be a Slippery Sam if he:

- Sweet-talks you after you find out he did something wrong
- Wants to know the details of your life and is secretive about his own
- Buys things for himself and doesn't tell you
- Is smooth and charming in public and at home when he is making up for something
- Tells little white lies and big fat black lies
- Maintains friendships with people you don't respect, then tells you to give them a chance
- He pushes off all responsibility for paying the bills (bills that he tends to run up) onto you, and then complains that you worry too much about money.
- Tells you that he'll do something but never does it
- Disappears for hours at a time and is vague about his whereabouts
- Blames you for your inability to trust him after he gives you reason not to trust him
- Calls you too suspicious or even paranoid after you don't believe his excuses

Remembering that he can't be spoiled without you spoiling him, you'll need to take a look at your part of it. Take this self-test:

1. After being outraged with him, do you warm up to him when he sweet-talks you?
   ○ Yes ○ No

2. Do you find yourself giving him the benefit of the doubt although the doubts are overwhelming?
   ○ Yes ○ No

3. Are there times when you feel so confused by his tangled excuses that you wonder if it's you who has the problem?
   ○ Yes ○ No

4. Do you make excuses for him to family and friends when he has done something you know was wrong?
   ○ Yes ○ No

5. Do you sometimes feel that he'll always reject your version of the truth and that the only way to survive in the relationship is to accept his version?
   ○ Yes ○ No

6. Do you look the other way when he overspends on himself?
   ○ Yes ○ No

7. Do you tell him what he wants to know if he asks you detailed questions about your whereabouts but is very hazy about his own?
   ○ Yes ○ No

8. If he uses the credit card as if it is available money without debt to worry about, do you do the worrying for him?
   ○ Yes   ○ No

9. Do you let his charm make up for everything?
   ○ Yes   ○ No

10. When he tells you that you worry too much about money, do you believe him?
    ○ Yes   ○ No

Add up the number of yes answers. The more yes answers, the greater your tendency to spoil him. Look at it another way: the greater your tendency to spoil him, the less chance there will be that he'll share the responsibility to meet you as an equal partner. This is because you're making it very hard for him not to expect you to make it easy on him.

SLIPPERY SAM, AKA *Entitled Man*, feels entitled to be taken care of and entitled to treat himself to the things he believes he deserves. He thinks he's even entitled to lie if it benefits him. His attitude is " I deserve the things I want, so why do I have to be accountable?" Where does that leave you?

You'll need to be on your toes with Slippery Sam to stop spoiling him. Turn to Chapter 11 for a detailed description of the tricks up his sleeve and what you can do to get him to grow up.

Magnificent Mike

Let's say that the man in your life is a Magnificent Mike. He expects you to have your emotions in order so that you can spend your time dealing with his. Heaven forbid that you should be upset or sad about something! This would be quite a nuisance for him, and it would take away from what he thinks should be your central focus: him.

You've got to trick him into getting beyond himself and joining you in a relationship, which is dependent on reciprocity. To transform Magnificent Mike into an equal partner, you have to get wise to his tricks. Here's how he gets you to spoil him:

- Claiming that he needs to be excused from making the same effort as you because he needs to preserve his energy for his special abilities
- Trying to convince you that filling his needs helps you, like trickle-down economics
- Referring to how other people appreciate and praise him, and how you ought to do the same
- Complaining about being tired and how much he's done on a special level even though he has done less than you
- Being unable to laugh at himself and expecting that you won't, either
- Demonstrating little sympathy for the truly needy
- Being unable to hear constructive criticism
- Acting generous only if there is a gain for him, then convinces you that there's a gain for you

If your man fits just one of these, then he has likely gotten the impression that you're easy to manipulate. If you fall for his tricks, you are as much to blame as he. Take this self-test:

1. Do you grant him special favors that he denies you?
   ○ Yes   ○ No

2. Do you honor his birthday while he hardly mentions yours?
   ○ Yes   ○ No

3. If you receive an accommodation—say, a first-class upgrade—do you tell him to take it?
   ○ Yes   ○ No

4. Do you allow him to get credit for something that you did for him?
   ○ Yes   ○ No

5. When he doesn't express praise for something you or somebody else does, do you let it slide because he was "distracted" by one of his "special projects"?
   ○ Yes   ○ No

6. Do you think of him as "high maintenance" while you know that he considers you no maintenance?
   ○ Yes   ○ No

7. Do you not laugh at him because he's unable to laugh at himself?
   ○ Yes   ○ No

8. Do you consistently feel that he has little sympathy for truly needy people, or for you when you're enduring something very difficult, and then tell yourself that you're imagining things?
   ○ Yes   ○ No

9. Do you let him make you feel guilty for not giving him more, even though you've given him too much?
   ○ Yes   ○ No

10. Do you hold back constructive criticism of him because he can't take it?
    ○ Yes   ○ No

Add up your score. If you answered yes to any of these questions, you're telling him that you don't matter. He is the center of the universe. You don't even merit planetary status. Consider yourself a mere moon.

> MAGNIFICENT MIKE IS *Center-of-the-Universe Man.* Your life revolves around him. He's probably always been the center of someone's universe and now he wants you to pay him the same homage. If he has to get up at 4 a.m. for an early flight, he believes that you will want to get up with him to see him off!

Magnificent Mike needs to be dealt with using a unique type of self-defense. Turn to Chapter 12 for a description of his tricks and how you can avoid giving in to his special needs.

Traditional Tom

Let's turn to Traditional Tom. There's a song in the play *Fiddler on the Roof* called "Tradition." The father of a young woman sings that he worries that she will forget tradition if she marries a modern man. Tradition can be a convenient excuse for a man to get you to spoil him.

It's hard to believe that not long ago women didn't have the right to vote in the United States. When the Constitution stated that all men are created equal, it didn't mean all humans. Unfortunately, even today in many societies and subcultures women play a subservient role to men. Whatever your culture, if a man can get you to go along with a traditional subservient role, he's got you in a major bind. He doesn't have to rely on his own tricks to get you to spoil him; he can simply say, "That's how it's always been."

I call a man who uses tradition Traditional Tom because he's in a time warp of tradition for tradition's sake. He's really using tradition because it supports his favored position. His all-too-convenient view of sex roles is traditional history in many societies. Your job is to invite him to join you in the twenty-first century.

Traditional Tom will get you to spoil him by referring to tradition. He challenges you to spoil him by convincing you to give him what other men get from their wives. He might even go one step further and point to passages in the Bible or another religious text that he claims verify his privileged position.

Before you can learn to unspoil him, you'll need to learn the types of tricks that he uses to get you to spoil him. The most common tricks used by Traditional Toms are:

- Making you feel morally wrong for putting your needs equal to his
- Making you feel at risk of isolation or being ostracized if you try to move away from your traditional sex role
- Maintaining that you have it easier than he does
- Patronizing you so you'll feel less equal
- Suggesting that to be pious is to serve him
- Claiming that there are sharp differences between men and women and that those differences favor men

Don't forget that he can't get away with all of those manipulations unless you believe them. Playing into any traps will spoil him. Take this self-test:

1. Do you believe that your needs are less important than his because you are a woman and need to support him?
   ○ Yes   ○ No

2. Do you do all the work to keep up with the maintenance of the household even though you hold down a job, too?
   ○ Yes   ○ No

3. Do you stay surrounded by friends and family who support his privileged position?
   ○ Yes   ○ No

4. Do you feel guilty if you ask (or even think about asking) him to do anything that he could call "women's work"?
   ○ Yes   ○ No

5. Do you support his belief that you have it easier than he does?
   ○ Yes   ○ No

6. When he says sexist things about women, do you tell him that you agree?
   ○ Yes   ○ No

7. Do you feel impious if you question his authority?
   ○ Yes   ○ No

8. When he subtly patronizes you, do you say something like, "Yes, honey"?
   ○ Yes   ○ No

9. Do you go along with his interpretations of religious text that support his position?
   ○ Yes   ○ No

10. Do you only socialize with people he approves of?
    ○ Yes   ○ No

Answering yes to any of the above questions tells him that you don't deserve to be treated as an equal partner. Since you state with your behavior that your job is to serve him, how can he resist being spoiled by you?

TRADITIONAL TOM, OR *Shrink-to-Fit Man*, wants a partner who will fit with his perspective. He thinks that because you are the woman, therefore the "weaker sex," you need his guidance. If you want to keep him happy, you'd better be ready to shrink to fit his idea of what that should be. He's going to try to form you like a lump of clay.

In Chapter 13, I'll further describe the tricks that Traditional Tom uses to get you to spoil him, and I'll show how you can get him to respect your equality. You'll learn how to make him join you in the twenty-first century as an equal partner.

Whatever type of spoiled man challenges you, change the rules. Don't respond by falling into his traps. Use the techniques I offer in the rest of the book. In the coming chapters I'll describe each type of spoiled man in detail and how you can avoid spoiling him. You'll learn how to use techniques to change your relationship and turn your man into an equal partner.

2 Unspoiling with the CODE

You've probably heard the Beatles song "All You Need Is Love." Maybe you've also heard Tina Turner's song "What's Love Got to Do With It?" Lily Tomlin said, "If love is the answer, could you rephrase the question?" The answer is that love isn't enough. You need more than love to keep your relationship healthy.

> OUR CULTURE WOULDN'T require divorce attorneys if "*all you need is love*" to make a relationship work. A couple certainly needs love, but more importantly, they need a satisfying level of compatibility to stay together.

The fast pace of daily life makes it too easy to forget the important parts of a healthy relationship. To make matters worse, when your man tries to get you to spoil him, you'll tend to forget those healthy parts even more easily. In this chapter, I'll describe the basic principles of a healthy relationship and contrast them with those followed by a spoiled man. To help you remember the healthy characteristics, I'll use one of the easiest-to-use memory techniques called the mnemonic. I've encoded them in the central mnemonic of the CODE: **C**ompassion, **O**penness, **D**epth, and **E**quality.

In the following story about Sara, notice how she tries to make decisions about her relationships based on what was healthy for her. She kept the CODE in mind as a definition of a healthy relationship.

SARA'S BIG CHOICE

Sara came to see me during a difficult transition in her life. Her husband had just left her for another woman. With encouragement she accepted invitations to dinner parties a few months after her divorce was final. Her friends wanted to introduce her to single men who were having a hard time meeting women.

Soon after the second dinner party she found herself pursued by two men, Karl and Joel.

She decided to accept both invitations but made it clear to them that she wanted to go slow with intimacy.

She found Karl to be very compassionate and open to hearing about the demise of her destructive marriage. He shared the history of his marriage and told her of the grief he felt when his wife died of cancer. At no point did Sara feel as though Karl was trying to pull her into feeling more sympathy for him than normal. He was not an especially handsome man but held a steady, if boring, job as a government bureaucrat.

Joel was the recipient of a large trust fund and didn't work. He took elaborate trips to expensive resorts. She fantasized that she would quit work and take trips with him. Since she went into debt after the divorce, she wondered if a relationship with him would mean getting out of debt. However, despite the riches, Joel was a pessimist and complained about all the people who had ever done him wrong, including his barber who had once given him a bad haircut.

One day she received a call from her doctor after a routine mammogram. He wanted to do a biopsy on a suspicious lump. That night she had dinner with Joel, who quickly made sure to keep the focus only as deep as his concerns. He said, "Even if you have cancer, your doctor will take care of it. So don't worry. Anyway, if you had my doctor there would be reason to worry. You know what he did to me. . . ."

She happened to have a lunch date with Karl the next day. He responded to her news by saying, "Oh, I'm so sorry. You must be very worried. Please let me drive you to the appointment." Later that day he called to check in with her.

After the lump was diagnosed as benign, she resumed seeing each of them once a week. However, something wasn't right and she couldn't put her finger on it.

At our next session Sara speculated that she hung onto Joel because of his wealth and good looks. There was little depth in her interest in him beyond those qualities. She decided that there was little room for equality in a relationship with Joel, so she told him that she needed "some time to sort things out" and didn't want to see him as much for awhile.

He responded by saying, "So, you're going to be just like the rest of them?"

Her first response was to feel guilty. Then she just sat there staring at him, wondering what he meant by "the rest of them." He waited for her to apologize. When she didn't, he said, "I guess you're just interested in yourself."

She felt instantly angered, then strangely relieved. She thought, how can he possibly be so stupid as to try to accuse me of selfishness?

During the next few weeks she continued to see Karl and he continued to show compassion, openness, and depth. He made her feel his equal, but she wasn't convinced that he was right for her yet.

One day he said, "This is so great that we are becoming close friends first . . . I mean before or if we become intimate."

She nodded, smiled, and said, "I'm glad you said 'if.' Let's see how it goes for awhile." Then she gave him a gentle kiss.

Sara had the general principles of a healthy relationship in mind when she parted ways with Joel. She was determined to work on cultivating a relationship with Karl based on the CODE that I describe below.

THE STEPS OF THE CODE

Here are the parts of the CODE and a brief list of ingredients:

1. **C**ompassion—empathy, generosity, patience, mutual warmth, and passion.
2. **O**penness—communication, honesty, receptivity, and flexibility.
3. **D**epth—increasing dimensionality, cultivating common interests, cultivating common values, and commitment.
4. **E**quality—mutual respect, balance, reciprocity, and shared rights.

Compassion

The first general principle of the CODE is **C**ompassion. It incorporates most of the qualities that love is composed of. The main parts of compassion include:

- Empathy
- Generosity
- Patience
- Warmth
- Passion

Let's take a closer look at some of these qualities.

Empathy

Empathy is the ability to feel and understand someone's plight and sympathize with him or her. Former President Clinton was famous for his ability to "feel the pain" of people in need of help. If you're like most people, you like to be understood, especially in your intimate relationship. When you are down or stressed, you appreciate it when your partner empathizes with you.

Empathy goes beyond sympathy. It's being able to put yourself in someone else's shoes. Spoiled men have a difficult time expressing empathy unless it's convenient for them. When they do, it might seem gratuitous.

IF HE IS spoiled, he may fail at empathy but be good at pretending. For instance, he might ask how your workday was, and you might answer "Terrible" and he might say "Sorry to hear that." When you look closely, you may notice that he's just saying what's expected. Look for a sign of insincerity in his face or tone of voice, and notice whether he quickly changes the subject to something he really cares about.

Generosity

Generosity means giving when there are no strings attached. It can be expressed as being generous with time, attention, or effort.

Giving is receiving. Unfortunately, a spoiled man often operates with the reverse philosophy, namely that giving means losing. Consequently, he's on the take. He pretends to be generous by reminding you of all the things that he's done for you. That's giving with strings attached. He acts generous when:

- He can get as much or more back in return.
- He will receive praise or recognition.
- There is an expectation to contribute and there are people around to witness that he met the expectation.
- It was pointed out that he hadn't contributed. At that point, he makes a gratuitous effort.

Spoiled men don't enjoy giving. To most people, it feels good to give because they understand how great the person receiving is feeling. Who wouldn't want someone to feel that happiness of receiving an expression of your love or respect? Many spoiled men don't feel happy for other people at the same level as generous people do. That's because they can't break out of their "me first" mindset.

Having real compassion means going out of your way to give of yourself. You don't give just because it's convenient or to get a payback. You don't hold back to see what's in it for you. There is no tit-for-tat. There is no scorecard.

Patience

The two of you probably move at different speeds, think at different depths, and react to events with different temperaments. It would be far easier for you if both of you were in sync all the time—but we all know that's not realistic. Since you're *not* always on the same page, you have a choice: either prod each other to change immediately or be patient with each other. It's critical that you are patient with one another because it allows you room to grow together. Patience means that you are accepting of one another.

If he's spoiled, he probably prods. He believes that you're on his schedule and that yours doesn't exist. Let's say you're getting ready to go somewhere. If you ask for his patience, he'll respond by:

- Sulking and grumbling that you're not ready
- Letting you do everything to prepare to go
- Taking his own sweet time after you're ready to go

Warmth

Warmth involves a comfortable and soothing feeling of being at home in the relationship. It allows tension to dissolve. *Each* of you should offer a peaceful, accepting, and relaxing tone to the other.

A spoiled man may fake warmth. When you are stressed or upset, he may even give you a hug. But within a few moments, he tenses up and you're back to his agenda: him. He may tell you how he is much *more* stressed or upset about something, thereby trying to shift the need for warmth back to him. You would probably not feel "at home" in the relationship.

Passion

Passion is more than intensified warmth. It is a part of what people call the "spark." It is heightened attention toward one another. Passion is more complete than mere eroticism. It can take many forms. It can be hot (sexy) or warm (not-as-sexy), but it probably mostly alternates in between. His healthy affectionate expressions of passion can include:

- Doing small favors for you that you didn't expect or ask for
- Picking up little gifts or flowers for you for no special reason
- Calling to find out how your day is going
- Affection, such as holding your hand and cuddling
- Erotic affection, such as kissing and making love

All of these are important. Don't get stuck making one of them more important than the others. The point is that affection should be part of the foundation of your relationship. It's one of the many ways of expressing your passion.

Spoiled men can also distort passion, however. A Slippery Sam can buy you gifts that break the budget. (He usually does this when trying to make up for something, including spending too much on himself.) And I've heard Magnificent Mikes say that they expect sex at least every other day. Although it's great that he wants you two to have a passionate relationship, you can't put a schedule on your lovemaking.

DOESN'T PHYSICAL AFFECTION involve a lot of understanding and compromising of both your and his individual needs? A spoiled man thinks his needs should be met when he wants and thinks part of your function in his life is to meet them. Sounds like he could use a wake-up call that you have needs, too.

Openness

The principle of openness may sound like a no-brainer to you. You may say, "Of course I hope he's open with me!" Unfortunately, it's not that simple.

There are basic principles to openness, which include:

- Communication
- Honesty
- Receptivity
- Flexibility

Let's examine these four principles further.

Communication

Clear communication is the fabric of a healthy relationship. Yet nobody communicates perfectly. In fact, much of human communication is based on *mis*understanding. Though both of you should try to resolve misunderstandings, making that effort is often a clumsy or awkward process. That's okay, though—what's important is that you do make a concerted attempt to communicate in a healthy and loving way, not that you resolve your problems as neatly as a half-hour sitcom does. Consistent effort helps clear up misunderstandings and makes your relationship more satisfying.

A spoiled man may not make an effort to communicate clearly. After all, he can get you to spoil him better if you make the effort *for* him. Or he may communicate with vibes, passivity, or guilt-tripping. He may use these methods to keep you off-balance and a little confused. If he participates in clear communication, he can't get you to spoil him as easily.

Honesty

Honesty involves transparency first and foremost. Your lives should be open to one another. Your friends can be his friends and his yours. You may have heard the saying "You can judge a person by the friends he keeps." If you can know his friends, you can know many sides of him.

You probably noticed that I used the word "can" when saying that you *can* know his friends. That's because it's a matter of choice. You can choose to not get very close to his friends for one reason or another. Maybe you have little in common with his friends. Maybe they live far away. But the fact that you can know them if you want to is important to the openness of your relationship. Openness means that neither of you hides parts of your lives.

DON'T YOU ENJOY hearing about someone's previous adventures or experiences in life? A spoiled man doesn't want you to talk about your past because he wasn't in it. He doesn't want to know the whole you, only the part of you that has to do with him here and now.

Receptiveness

Who both of you were in the past is part of who you are in the present. But if he's a Traditional Tom, he'd better not hear about anyone before him! If he's a Passive Pete, he won't tell you about his past, but he sure will make you feel guilty about asking. If he is a Magnificent Mike, he may not want to hear about your past because your life should begin with him. And if he's a Slippery Sam, he's open to your past, but there may be parts of his that he doesn't want you to hear about. Since knowing who he was in the past helps you know him in the present, if he won't talk about his past you are left wondering what he's hiding. Alternatively, he may misrepresent his past.

His reluctance to give you a clear picture of his past implies that:

- He is worried that you may find out that he hasn't been trustworthy in the past.
- He doesn't want you to know that he can repeat past undesirable behavior.

How receptive he is to *your* past is a measure of how much he can appreciate you as a complete person. A spoiled man needs you to feel incomplete without him.

Flexibility

A healthy, open relationship requires that you are flexible with one another. Since we are all imperfect beings and nothing ever turns out the way we expect, flexibility gives your relationship durability. Flexibility acts like shock absorbers on your relationship, absorbing the bumpy parts on the road of life.

A spoiled man can be inflexible. He wants all the compromise to come from you and he wants things his way. If things don't work out the way he wanted, or your shortcomings contributed to things not working out, he'll make you feel bad about it. This bind is meant to keep you on the defensive and feeling that you are always accountable to him.

Depth

A healthy relationship is a world within itself. Though not closed off from the world around it, the relationship should provide each of you with an enriched home base to grow together. You can increase or stunt the depth in your relationship by things you do together. Ideally, both of you cultivate depth in your relationship by:

- Increasing the dimensions of the relationship
- Cultivating intellectual rapport
- Enhancing emotional rapport
- Harmonizing values
- Honoring your commitment

Depth Through Variety

As you expand the range of activities and interests that you share, so, too, do you expand the depth of your relationship. If, on the other hand, you only participate in routine activities such as going to movies that he wants to see, eating at restaurants he wants to go to, or watching television shows that he chooses, your relationship stays one-dimensional—his dimension.

Each of you should have a say in what you do and whom you see. The more variation you have in your life together, the more dimension you provide to your relationship. A deep relationship is fresh and alive, not stale and stiff. The variety of things that you do together does not need to be excessive or the people you see dramatic. These things may be relaxing, such as sitting together in a mountain park or meeting with friends for lunch.

Depth Through Emotional Rapport

If he expects you to adjust to his moods but does little to adjust to yours, the relationship lacks emotional rapport. Under these conditions, a spoiled man dictates the emotional climate in the relationship. If you go along with his emotional weather patterns, you're asking for more of them.

You are both emotional creatures who react to events in your lives with all sorts of emotions, depending on the situation. When you each make an effort to understand how the other responds emotionally to life's events, you'll enhance your emotional rapport with each other.

If you find yourself adjusting to his emotions while he disregards yours, you're not enhancing emotional rapport—you're coddling a spoiled man. You can't do all the work! Enhancing emotional rapport can only occur if both of you try. The two of you need this rapport, and if you don't have it, you'll feel like there's something fundamentally wrong.

Emotional depth develops after the "honeymoon" phase of your relationship. The infatuation you feel for each other at first fuels the magical feeling of falling in love. Soon, both of you realize that the other is but a mortal with flaws. Then that infatuation withers away. But your relationship doesn't have to sour like many do after the honeymoon period just because the excitement of novelty evaporates. Hopefully, it will deepen and gain satisfying emotional rapport.

> KEEP YOUR RELATIONSHIP interesting and vital. The fire of the first months will not be blazing anymore, so it's time to cultivate mutual interests. Take a class together, develop a hobby, or read some of the same books.

Depth in a lasting relationship is not sensational, but subtle. It's the appreciation for the subtle aspects of your relationship that can move it beyond the early excitement of infatuation. Strive to spend some quiet time together—walking together, watching the sunset, or working in the garden together.

FEWER COUPLES ARE getting married, and in many states over 50 percent of marriages end in divorce. The divorce rate has doubled since 1960. We live harried lives in a high-pressure society, and we suffer from a lack of depth and commitment in our intimate relationships. Despite all this, we as a society have also made positive advancements in relationship health. For example, fifty years ago, couples often stayed together despite gross incompatibility. Today, both partners expect fulfillment. The growth of marriage seminars and counseling services testify to the increased importance of compatibility. So we are *trying* to make our relationships better!

Depth Through Common Values

"Values" are often a hot topic on contentious political talk shows and in candidates' debates. But values are a lot more than political currency. Real values are personal, ethical, compassion-based, and philosophical.

By cultivating mutually respected values, you and your mate will instill integrity and depth in your relationship. Mutually respected values are beliefs that you either share or agree that you respect in each other. I emphasize the word *mutual*, because if you focus just on his values, you'll spoil him. Traditional Tom, for example, wants you to focus on his values, especially those values that place him in a privileged position.

A healthy relationship involves sharing your thoughts, feelings, and values. Since values without intellect are hollow at best and destructive at worst, you'll need to keep your relationship's brain-power alive by bouncing ideas off one another. In other words, think about what you believe and be prepared to debate so that your beliefs can mature. In some relationships with Traditional Toms, values hollow out or become destructive if he feels that the depth of intellectual discussion can threaten his favored position.

Depth Through Commitment

Another way to achieve depth is through commitment. You may find the term *commitment* to be very general and perhaps even confusing. Being committed to each other means that both of you have decided that your relationship is a priority. Your relationship is not a matter of convenience, it's a matter of devotion toward each other. It will probably be tested by any number of stressors, but with commitment and loyalty your relationship can weather any storm.

Loyalty means he's there when it counts. Far from being a fair-weather partner, when you are challenged by others he is there to support you. His principal alliance should be with you because you two are a team. If he vowed that he would be monogamous, then his faithfulness to that vow represents his commitment to you.

A spoiled man, however, may take his vowed commitment lightly. If he is a Slippery Sam, for example, he may flirt with other women and make you wonder about his faithfulness. If he is a Magnificent Mike, he may expect you to be more loyal to him than he is to you.

A Passive Pete may simply not make the effort to show you his commitment if there's a potential loss to him. For example, let's say that you're at a party together and you need him to volunteer feedback because you are getting in a tight spot where you might embarrass yourself by saying something that is not true. Being loyal to you involves trying to help you pull back from such a comment in a supportive and uncritical way. If he doesn't make the effort and fails to give you that support and feedback because he might come under scrutiny, then his commitment is in question.

Equality

Equality sets a strong, level foundation on which your relationship is built. If your relationship isn't rooted in equality, it is doomed to fall apart. It would be like trying to build a house of cards on a mountain slope.

Equality has four dimensions:

1. Mutual respect
2. Balance
3. Reciprocity
4. Shared rights

Mutual Respect

Each of you should bring unique talents, aptitudes, and sensitivities to the relationship. Respecting each other for those contributions gives you equal stature. Since you are different from each other, you'll need to respect each other's differences as well as your similarities.

Perhaps you have used the clichés "my other half" or "my soulmate" to describe your partner. Those overidealized concepts aren't particularly useful in most cases, but they do metaphorically describe how you two can complement one another in ever-changing circumstances.

I use the word *incomplete* to point out that perfect balance is a myth. We all are flawed. Even in the healthiest of relationships, you will experience friction and ongoing adjustments as you evolve and grow together. If you overcompensate for his shortcomings and he doesn't do the same for you, there's no equality in the relationship.

You can complement one another by accepting and respecting each other's limitations and skills. Let's say you're a very talented chef and good at getting people from diverse backgrounds to find commonalities. You put on wonderful dinner parties. But if he's a Passive Pete, he may sit back and not only let you cook, but passively rely on your gregarious social skills to make the dinner party enjoyable. All the work that you put into the preparation of the meal needs to be offset by him not only making an active effort to contribute socially, but also by cleaning up after the meal.

PERFECTION IS a myth. You recognize that you are not truly perfect, right? Have you ever met anyone who is? No. Then why do we unrealistically expect two imperfect people to equal one perfect relationship? That doesn't make the slightest bit of sense. What does make sense is working to develop and maintain a *better* relationship.

Balance

Balance in your relationship can shift back and forth like a seesaw. When you're stressed out, support should shift back to you. If both of you are experiencing stress, you need to support one another. Balance should reflect your equal importance.

A spoiled man expects every tip in your direction (if he allows one) to be compensated by two tips in his direction. Yet equality doesn't involve a tit-for-tat scorecard. Rigid accounting of who gets what is not only unrealistic but also builds in micromanagement that can undermine your relationship. As I pointed out earlier, giving with an expectation of receiving is not real giving.

Reciprocity

Equality must include flexible reciprocity. The give and take is not a question of whether the reciprocity is immediate and in the same form—if he rubs your back, you don't have to automatically rub his back. There may no reason for him to get his back rubbed at that moment or even soon thereafter. His "back rub" may not even come in the form of a back rub—it may come in another helpful form. The things that you do for one another shouldn't come at a prescribed time or only for a compulsory payback, because then they'll feel forced. These efforts should occur randomly and often.

You won't find much reciprocity in a relationship with a spoiled man. Though he may claim to want reciprocity, he actually doesn't because he would lose his upper hand. With you paying attention to his needs and forgetting your own, he has it made.

> WOMEN FOUGHT LONG and hard for equality. So why should you give up on it in your relationship? His neediness is no reason for you to set aside equality.

Shared Rights

The classic novel *Animal Farm* by George Orwell has a line that describes how people can distort equal rights. The social organization among the animal community adopted the concept "All animals are equal but some animals are more equal than others."

A spoiled man pretends to share equal rights with you. But when it comes down to practice, he thinks his rights are more equal than yours. He thinks he has more of a right to complain than you do and the right to more sympathy than you, and since he's a master at getting you to take care of him, you put his needs first. Though he may pay lip service to your needs, he thinks his right to emotional support is more important than yours.

You must truly share the same rights for equal attention, support, and time to feel like a whole human being before being obligated to respond to his needs, real or imagined. Again, without equality, your relationship is lopsided and doomed to fail, so make sure that you have an even foundation for it to stabilize and grow.

SUMMING UP THE CODE

When he tries to get you to spoil him, it's very easy to get frustrated and forget what it takes to maintain a healthy relationship. Use the mnemonics of the CODE to remember the basic characteristics of a healthy relationship: Compassion, Openness, Depth, and Equality. If your relationship drifts away from the CODE, you're drifting away from a healthy relationship.

Settle for nothing less than the CODE and make sure both of you share an appreciation for its principles. However, don't do all the work to follow the CODE while he goes along for the ride. Both partners need to participate to make a healthy relationship. Your emotional reaction to his laziness will undermine the foundation of your relationship and your sense of well-being. In the next chapter, I'll describe how this happens and how you can avoid it.

After each chapter you'll find a little quiz to review what you learned. Don't worry about how you do on them. These quizzes are meant to be both fun and a way to review the main points of each chapter. The quiz questions are in a multiple-choice format. Some answers are ridiculous and others are the opposite of what you need to do. You'll find an answer key at the back of the book to check how well you did.

CHAPTER 2

checkup quiz
Unspoiling with the CODE

1. If he demands compassion from you but offers none in return:
   a. Give him what he wants because at least one of you can benefit from compassion.
   b. Balance your expression of compassion with reminders of consequences of his actions and the limits of your tolerance.
   c. Try to make your compassion win him over.
   d. Tell him that he's a cold bastard.

2. If he says that he feels compassion for you but behaves as if he has none:
   a. Let him know that you need to be convinced by his behavior that he means what he says.
   b. Tell him that his words are soothing to hear.
   c. Assume that he hasn't yet figured out how to express it, and cut him some slack.
   d. Believe that it's good he's at least saying it and that you shouldn't be so ungrateful.

3. If he peppers you with all sorts of questions and offers no answers to yours:
   a. Answer his questions because he is interested in you.
   b. Ask him why he doesn't answer questions.
   c. Answer none of his questions.
   d. Wonder what he is hiding.

4. If he acts offended when hearing about previous boyfriends or an ex-husband:
   a. Keep them all secret and maintain little shrines for them.
   b. Ask one of them over for dinner to help him get over it.
   c. Be sensitive to his feelings but not secretive.
   d. Feel guilty about your past and repent!

5. When he tries to keep the focus on his petty concerns:
   a. Work to cultivate depth by focusing on common interests while ignoring his petty concerns.
   b. Stay as deep as his petty concerns until he gets tired of them.
   c. Assume that he only has the capacity for pettiness, not depth, so don't expect anything more.
   d. Ask him to teach you to be petty, too.

6. If he tells you that you aren't satisfied with the way "things are" and that he's a "simple man":
   a. Say you'd like to cultivate a deeper connection.
   b. Just accept that he's a simpleton.
   c. Limit your interests and become a "simple woman."
   d. Cultivate an appetite for sour milquetoast.

7. If he treats you like a second-class citizen:
   a. Consider the wisdom of his class consciousness.
   b. Let him know clearly and consistently that this is not an arrangement that you'll accept.
   c. Treat him like a third-class citizen.
   d. Do your best to care for the master.

8. If he pays lip service to women's rights outside the home but at home you feel unequal:
   a. Figure that at least outside the house he supports equality.
   b. Praise him for his sense of equality.
   c. Ask him to practice what he preaches.
   d. Keep his secret well.

9. If he acts warm and compassionate but makes no effort to seek depth in your relationship:
   a. Be satisfied with what you have.
   b. Tell him that one way he can express his compassion for you is to cultivate depth.
   c. Tell him that he's a shallow blob of emotions.
   d. Try to get depth from other relationships.

10. If he's open with you about your respective pasts but seems to put you in a one-down position:
    a. Be open with him about your past so that he can properly evaluate it.
    b. Tell him you would appreciate it if he could refrain from turning your confidences into reasons to criticize you.
    c. Shut down and tell him that you don't measure up to him.
    d. Do your best to stroke his ego because it looks like he needs it.

3

Seeing Red Flags

As you drive down a road riddled with potholes, falling rocks, or hairpin turns, you count on warning signs to alert you to the conditions of the road ahead. Your relationship is like a road. You don't know for sure what's ahead as you progress, but are there any warning signs?

Many women have told me that they "would have given anything to have known he was like that!" They find out that there were early signs, but they realize this too late in their relationship. They say they missed clues about him that were obvious to their family and friends.

AN EXPERIENCED TEACHER starts the school year laying down the ground rules for students. These rules are firm and clear with little flexibility. Like that teacher, begin your relationship with clearly articulated expectations. If you don't like a behavior, don't remain quiet. It will never go away on its own accord; in fact, it will become worse.

In this chapter, you'll learn about how to identify the warning signs that you are drifting into a relationship with a man who wants you to spoil him. We can call those signs "red flags," signaling dangerous territory ahead. Notice in the story below how Pam learned to pay attention to red flags, and because of this made pivotal shifts in her relationship with Peter.

PETER AND PAM

After Pam graduated from college, she moved back home with her parents. Not only did she become bored and lonely, but she began to worry that she would fall too quickly into a relationship that was unhealthy because of it. That's when she came in for counseling.

She told me that she had met Peter at a mutual friend's birthday party and had gone away feeling that it had been a magical evening. Peter called the next day to ask her out on a date. The night of the date seemed to glow like a euphoric dream, as did the next five dates.

She told me that he seemed to be everything she wanted him to be. He worked hard to demonstrate that he wasn't like other men whose eyes would glaze over when she talked about her day; he tried to be totally present for her.

The Sunday after our second session, they were scheduled to go to a concert that she had bought tickets for and was really looking forward to attending.

That morning he called, saying, "I'm sorry, I totally forgot that I promised to go over to Jim's place to help him lay carpet in his den."

She was disappointed, but she understood that it was a mistake that he was apologizing for.

While out to dinner a few nights later, they ran into his friend Jim.

"Hey Bro," Jim said. "Good game last Sunday!"

Peter glanced uneasily at her, and then tried to cover his

embarrassed expression. He turned back to Jim. "Oh sure, yeah, uh. See you later."

At our next session, she reflected on the fact that she had been lonely before meeting him and spoke of being worried that she would risk losing the relationship over such a minor thing as questioning him about his friend's comment on the football game. Yet with encouragement she decided that it would be healthy to ask him about it. She confronted him about his friend's comment and the last-minute canceling of their date. It caught him off guard because she wove her question into the context of the conversation they were having about something else. Then she said, "Next time you cancel on me like that, please don't do it on the day of the event."

Within a week, he gave her a chance to respond to another red flag. As they were finishing dinner at her house, he drifted into the living room and turned on the television.

"What are you doing?" she asked.

"Oh, just wanted to check the score on the game."

"And leave me to clean up?"

He looked stunned. "No, uh, I was going to do the dishes because you did the cooking."

"I want to be treated with respect and not taken for granted."

"I don't take you for granted!"

"You'll have to prove that over time." And she meant it. At any sign of even a hint of a red flag she asked for an immediate explanation.

You can learn how to see warning signs so that you can make pivotal shifts in your relationship—early on like Pam did, or later in your relationship as will be discussed further on in this chapter. These warning signs can be bright red flags like the ones Pam noticed or they can be harder to see. To get yourself to stop spoiling him, you need to be alert to red flags of all types and shades.

TAKE THESE STEPS

1. Be alert to red flags warning of things he does that cry out for you to spoil him.
2. Be alert to the red flags signaling things you do in response to his spoiled behavior.
3. Be alert to the internal red flags represented by the mnemonic TRAP (see below).
4. Use these feelings of being TRAPped to stir yourself into action.

Your feelings can serve as a weathervane that alerts you of a storm in your relationship. The mnemonic TRAP corresponds to feelings that may well up inside of you when you deal with spoiled behavior: Tension, Resentment, Anger, and Powerlessness. When these feelings occur together, they erode your sense of self. Remember TRAP, and use it as a tool to remind yourself that you're spoiling him.

When you experience all of the TRAPped feelings at the same time, you're more vulnerable to his tricks because having these feelings together makes you confused and off-balance. Each of these four feelings is a red flag that waves energetically, demanding that you pay attention to its message: It's time to change how you respond to him.

If you ignore these internal red flags, he'll take advantage of you and you'll become even more vulnerable to the tricks he uses to get you to spoil him. That's because you'll be so overwhelmed with these TRAPped emotions that you'll be off-balance. Eventually the relationship can become so lopsided that it can be difficult to regain equality.

If you miss the red flags along the way, the situation will get worse. Pam caught them early. Had she not, she would have cultivated a spoiled man, which would have required that she work doubly hard to change the relationship later on.

SHADES OF RED FLAGS

Though red flags come in all shades of red, none of them should be ignored. Here are red flags of various shades:

- You hear your friends and family point out his bad characteristics and feel that they just haven't seen his good side yet.
- He has made the same apology about the same transgression several times.
- Despite the fact that you asked him not to do something, he did it anyway.
- You have TRAPped emotions that tell you something is wrong.

If it's early in your relationship, he may try to put his best foot forward because he doesn't want to risk scaring you away. He wants to entice you, to woo you with his sensitivity and generosity. But if he doesn't try as hard as you do and you tell yourself that he will later, you're lying to yourself. Maybe it's the best you're going to see. This may mean that you're going to see much worse to come; it could be just the tip of the iceberg of how spoiled he can be.

Later in your relationship, red flags are more difficult to see. They may not appear to you to be anything close to red, or you may become color-blind. Perhaps you see white flags instead of red because he always apologizes profusely. Or perhaps you see green flags when you find (or can think of) an innocent explanation for what you perceived as thoughtlessness.

Pam could have seen a green flag if Peter had told her that after he and his friend had put in the carpet he was asked to watch the football game. The green flag is that Peter is a good friend—someone who lends a hand. After all, who wouldn't want a boyfriend who is generous with his time and energy?

If you look at all the flags strung out over time, you may find that the haze and fog begin to lift. What was once a blur of color turns out to be just red flags waving brightly in the emotional climate of your relationship.

If you don't change how you respond to those red flags, they will turn into black flags. You'll sink deeper into quicksand and may begin to feel that it's impossible to change the relationship. Though it's never too late, the sobering reality is that the longer you wait to change your relationship, the more difficult it will be. Look at it another way: Patterns are easier to break if they are just beginning; once a rut develops, it gets deeper every time you repeat the bad behavior. Your job is to break out of it as soon as you see red flags and feel TRAPped.

A spoiled man can stir up a lot of emotions within you, and few of them are pleasant emotions. Take a Slippery Sam, for example. You're going to be **T**ense if he's keeping you on your toes wondering what he has up his sleeve. So, you may cut him some slack because your toes get tired. As you rest back on your heels he spends money on himself behind your back or lies about something. You become **R**esentful seeing how he gets you to spoil him.

Say he's a Passive Pete and his lack of effort and absence of enthusiasm throws a wet blanket over everything you do together. You're tired of feeling like you have to encourage him to participate all the time. It becomes emotionally exhausting to try to fill his bottomless emotional pit. As the **A**nger builds up, it should serve as a red flag that something is deeply wrong in your relationship.

Let's say he's a Magnificent Mike who insists on special favors from you and never returns any. Doesn't that get you incredibly angry? If you're not careful, he can use your anger against you. So you suppress it, and as a result you feel **P**owerless.

The most ominous emotional red flag is when you feel a sense of powerlessness when you are with him. You feel that no matter what you do, you're stuck in a no-win situation. A Traditional Tom may make you feel powerless because he has family and friends backing his favored position over you.

TYPES OF RED FLAGS

Since there are different phases of your relationship, the types of red flags you'll see will differ over time. They will also vary depending on the type of partner you have. For example, it's hard to notice red flags during the early part of your relationship. We can call the flag that you see then a green flag. If he is especially needy and you are tricked into thinking that he needs to be taken care of, we can call that a camouflaged flag. If he is very passive, like Passive Pete, we can say that you may see white flags. If you have a Slippery Sam and don't know what he is doing, we can call that an invisible flag.

The "honeymoon phase" is characterized by the sensationalism and superficiality endemic in our culture. Just as many movies neglect plots requiring reflection and thought in favor of dazzling special effects, both of you run the risk of fixating on the excitement and new feeling of your relationship without giving it the reflection and thought it may require. Consequently, you can be color-blind and can misperceive red flags for green flags. In other words, he may seem to be truly in need of your support when he really is only seeking attention.

FALLING IN LOVE could be better described as falling into infatuation. This phase is not falling into the fullness of love. Love involves an appreciation for all the parts of you including your flaws. Infatuation is the appreciation of one dimension, your best side. Inherent in this simplistic mindset is the idea that love occurs on its own accord or as if through some act of God. Love can be subtle. Infatuation is sensational.

Work toward surviving the infatuation phase with your color vision intact. When he catches on to the fact that you are fallible, he may want to leave the relationship for another ideal one. What he doesn't realize is that ideal mates exist only in fantasy.

The transition from the honeymoon part of your relationship to being a long-term couple should be guided by the principles of CODE. As you cultivate the CODE, look out for red flags, because, as in Pam's situation, sometimes those red flags are difficult to see in the early part of your relationship and they can be easy to miss.

Red flags may be triggered by the sorts of things he does or says. Peter, for example, claimed to have been obligated to help a friend put in carpet as an excuse to avoid going to a concert with Pam. Had Pam been slow in recognizing red flags as they occurred, she probably would have begun to have TRAPped feelings. Those feelings would serve as internal red flags, signaling to her that something was wrong and that she needed to pay attention.

After the infatuation phase of your relationship passes, both of you will probably come to realize that you're mortals with flaws and limitations. If he tries to get you to make up for your flaws by spoiling him while he doesn't reciprocate, that's a big red flag.

Red flags can show up at any point in relationships. Because cultivating the CODE in your relationship requires sustained effort, there's always the risk that one or both of you may not try as hard as you did in the beginning. If he tends toward being spoiled, he won't try as hard as you.

When you pick up the slack and try for him, that's not just a red flag for you but also a big signal to him that you aim to spoil him. When TRAPped feelings come up as you pick up the slack, this should signal to you that it's time to take a look at the kind of things you're doing to spoil him.

CAMOUFLAGED RED FLAGS

He may seduce you into thinking that his neediness can't be helped. This is a red flag camouflaged as a green flag. Once again, perfecting your color vision requires that you keep focused on the CODE. If his neediness conflicts with the CODE and it's actually a red flag because he's truly not in need, then he just wants you to spoil him.

I've heard countless men say "I fell out of love with her" or "She's not the woman I thought she was." This kind of statement can come up if you're late in responding to red flags. In this sense, he's right that you're no longer going to spoil him and that he got too comfortable with you spoiling him. In fact, from a simplistic point of view, he had a great deal. Why wouldn't he be confused and angry if things changed?

Many a spoiled man gets upset when you stop spoiling him. He'll use all sorts of tactics to get you to think his neediness is legitimate. If you don't start spoiling him again, he'll reach a pivotal position. He must choose whether to move ahead into a healthy relationship or threaten to leave it. If you allow yourself to be manipulated by his threat, then you're right back where you started—spoiling him again.

Your challenge is to stay firmly committed to the CODE and consider comments such as "You've changed" as a red flag signaling how far away from a healthy relationship you have drifted. You'll need to get back on course to a healthy relationship, and being alert to red flags will help you do that.

He may also find it difficult to accept the fact that you may need his support or extra effort during stressful periods. If he shifts the focus back to himself, consider that a red flag. He may try to convince you that his stress is greater than yours. This is not a green flag but a bright red one.

Look out for red flags that flap wildly in the breeze when his image of you as the perfect mate is damaged because you are temporarily experiencing an emotional low. Perhaps you're stressed out and become anxious, distracted, or even irritable. Say he wants to go to a party, but you're sad because you lost your job. He might tell you to suck it up and go without you. That's a big red flag. Or maybe you're sad about a loss or family problems. Whatever your emotional climate may be, it is part of you. Being in a relationship with you should include all of you, even your symptoms of stress and sadness. If you hide those feelings, you're spoiling him. Resist pretending you're perfect.

SUMMING UP RED FLAGS

Paying attention to red flags will help you make sure that you don't find yourself in the quicksand of spoiling him. Sometimes red flags come from external events, such as what he does or doesn't do. Sometimes they come from feelings that get stirred up within you—feelings of tension, resentment, anger, and powerlessness (TRAP). If you don't resolve the problems signaled by red flags, you'll be overwhelmed by TRAPped feelings while you spoil him.

Your plan should be to pay attention to both external red flags (triggered by what he does) and internal red flags (triggered by what you feel). Use those TRAPped feelings to stir yourself into action.

CHAPTER 3

checkup quiz
Seeing Red Flags

1. When your friends and relatives tell you they have noticed that you do many things for him that he could do for himself:
   a. Tell them to mind their own business.
   b. Explain to them that he really needs your help.
   c. Shrug it all off as them being overly critical.
   d. Look for the patterns that they point out.

2. If he tells you that you don't trust him when you catch him being fast and loose with the facts:
   a. Give him the credit that he asks for.
   b. Give him the credit that he has earned.
   c. Wonder if you're misreading him.
   d. Feel guilty that he thinks that you aren't giving him credit.

3. When you feel tense when he grows quiet and sullen:
   a. Assume you said something to hurt him.
   b. Do your best to get him in a better mood.
   c. Regard that tension as an intuitive feeling that he is trying to get you to feel responsible for something.
   d. Keep changing the subject until you feel less tension and he begins to talk.

4. When you begin to feel overwhelmed with resentment and can't put your finger on why you feel resentment:
   a. Watch for peaks and valleys of feeling resentment as you interact with him to identify what is causing the resentment.
   b. Feel ungrateful for everything that he's done for you.
   c. Tell him that you're sorry for not appreciating him as you should.
   d. Override those feelings of resentment by spoiling him even more.

5. If you feel overwhelmed with anger when he passively sits back and lets you do all the work:
   a. Unleash your anger in a tirade.
   b. Try to quiet your anger so that he won't be bothered by it.
   c. Consider the anger as a sign that it is time to adopt a different strategy to change your relationship, such as splitting up the chores.
   d. Consider the anger a bad emotion and feel ashamed of yourself.

6. If you feel powerless to change his spoiled behavior:
   a. Think it's a confirmation that the situation is hopeless.
   b. Think it's a confirmation that you're contributing to his spoiled behavior.
   c. Go along with what he wants because it's easier.
   d. Sink into a depression in the hope that he may take pity on you.

7. When you feel tension, anger, and powerlessness:
    a. Allow these feelings to make you feel overwhelmed and incapacitated.
    b. Channel the TRAPped feelings into fuel for changing your relationship.
    c. Tell him that you feel all these feelings and that it's up to him to decide what to do.
    d. Think there's something wrong with you and keep it hidden from him.

8. When he gives you a negative response to your plans all the time and you feel TRAPped:
    a. Get negative with him and see how he likes it.
    b. Offer new plans so that you can escape feeling that way.
    c. Stop your efforts and tell him why in a calm voice.
    d. Sit patiently and listen to his negative comments.

9. When you feel stressed or upset about something and need support but he offers barely a few words:
    a. Feel guilty about bothering him with your needs.
    b. Seek out a friend who is receptive and supportive.
    c. Pretend that his few gratuitous words of support did the trick.
    d. Get quiet and feel horrible.

10. If he tells you that you'll be there to pick up the pieces if he fails at something you have warned against:
    a. Pick up the pieces just as he expects you to.
    b. Tell him beforehand that you won't pick up the pieces, then do it anyway.
    c. Consider this a wake-up call as to the degree to which you have been spoiling him.
    d. Let the pieces fall in your lap then feel terrible.

PART TWO

roles men take
to get you
to *spoil* them

4

Challenging the Victim

One of the ways that a spoiled man can entice you into paying attention to his needs (and forget your own!) is to play the role of the victim. This is an especially powerful way to get your attention and make you think that his neediness is justified.

Most people feel sorry for true victims of injustice and trauma. It's normal to want to protect and take care of them. However, a spoiled man knows that you'll have this reaction to a victim-like *character* as well, so he plays the victim in order to get you to spoil him. He keeps you off-balance because he knows that you're not going to be critical of him and give him reason to be a victim, nor will you demand an equal effort during a time of need when he is in a victim role. Instead, you'll tend to take care of and nurture him because he's wounded and needs your support.

TRUE VICTIM OR ACTOR?

The truth is, you don't know if he's really a victim or just playing the part. A spoiled man can play victim with such expertise that he can demand sympathy and elicit feelings of guilt from you. When you aren't sympathetic to his victim status, he encourages you to believe that you're his victimizer. In this chapter, you'll learn to escape and deflect this unwarranted blame.

The following story about Beverly will illustrate how, after many years of marriage, she learned to escape responsibility for her husband's victim role. Though emotionally fatigued from being the "strong one," she was able to eventually confront him and turn things around.

ALAN AND BEVERLY

Beverly came in for counseling complaining that after thirty years of marriage she found herself emotionally exhausted. She acknowledged that she let her husband, Alan, play the victim role from the very beginning of their relationship. She told me that even on their first date she saw red flags that should have clued her to a distinct pattern. Alan always seemed to make it a point to bring up at least one person who had done him an injustice. Sometimes it was the airline ticketing agent who was just a "little too brusque." Other times, it was coworkers who had left him too much extra work.

Beverly's First Red Flags

On their third date, a teenager behind the ticketing booth at the theater asked him to repeat the name of the movie for which Alan was purchasing tickets. He repeated the title twice. Beverly knew there was a lot of noise in the line, but he didn't bother to lean up to the window so the young man could hear him better.

On the way into the theater after finally purchasing the tickets, he said, "They ought to fire kids like that! It ruins the atmosphere."

The movie was a comedy but he was not in a mirthful mood as they walked out of the theater. He glared at the ticket booth. The teenager was gone but Alan wasn't finished with him. "I hope they came to their senses and fired him."

She thought for a moment that he must be joking, then chose a relevant line from the movie. "That's life," she laughed.

As they got into the car he asked, "What are you laughing at?"

She looked at him, trying to decide what he meant. Then she smiled and said, "The movie. 'That's life.' Get it?"

He stared at her, looking as though he was trying to decide what she was actually saying. "Yeah, right. It was an okay movie. How about next Friday night?"

She had planned on visiting her mother, so she said, "I've got plans. How about Saturday instead?"

"Plans?" he said, as if he were hurt. She had the distinct impression that he wanted to ask her if she was seeing someone else.

"My mother is ill."

He hung his head as if to say that he didn't believe her and assumed that he was being rejected.

But how could he? She had offered Saturday night as an alternative. Then came the big red flag.

Beverly's Big Red Flag

You could say that this red flag hit Beverly over the head.

"Maybe you could visit her on Saturday instead and we could go out on Friday," he said less as a question than a statement. "Otherwise I wouldn't see you for more than a whole week. I'd be kinda lonely. That is, unless it's someone other than your mother?"

"I said my mother is ill. I told her I'd help her out around the house," she said.

"Oh, I thought she had a cold or something," he said, still

looking unconvinced that they were really talking about her mother.

She wanted to say that even though it wasn't serious, it was her mother and she was expecting help. Instead, she said, "You're right, it's just a cold. I'll change my plans."

"Good, I'll pick you up around six, if that's okay?"

She told me that for years to come, she regretted going out with him that night. She went on to describe a long history of incidents, some large, mostly small, where she adjusted her plans because he played the victim. He was a cross between Passive Pete and Traditional Tom.

The Vacation

Beverly and I worked on how she could effectively deal with his victim role. She wanted to develop a strategy before they took their grandchildren on a family cruise. It's a good thing she did, because when she returned from the trip she told me that he had played the victim role more than usual. In this vacation story, notice the strategy that she uses to keep Alan from inciting her pity by playing the victim role.

Everything was going smoothly until he somehow lost his wallet and credit cards in one of the busy, crowded port towns. When he got back on board he sulked around blaming the cruise line, the town, the captain, and even Beverly!

When his beaming grandson asked him, "Isn't this cool, Grandpa? Aren't you having fun?" Alan responded negatively with "No, I'm not. Why is that island part of the cruise? The streets are mobbed and there is nothing to buy but crap."

That turned the heads of several people on the deck nearby. She managed to be charming and apologetic to the fellow passengers, excusing him by telling them about how much he wanted this trip to be perfect for the grandkids and now he felt he let them down.

Alan stomped off mumbling to himself, "The trip is ruined."

Beverly's Confrontation

Beverly saw that his behavior was confusing to their young grandchildren and decided to talk to him about it if it continued. He was unable to shake off the attitude, and his victim behavior began to color the trip even more. Finally, at dinner the next evening, the grandkids looked noticeably glum because Grandpa was still in a bad mood. When the younger one began to miss her parents and cried at bedtime, suddenly Beverly saw how his victim behavior was victimizing the grandchildren they both loved so dearly. She decided that this was the time to confront him.

She said to him, "If the trip is ruined for you, then that's the way it is for you. But your attitude is not going to ruin it for the kids. Why don't you consider getting off at the next port and flying home?"

He looked mortally wounded. For a moment she felt that she should apologize. Then he mumbled, "How could you be so insensitive?"

"Who is the one being so insensitive, Alan? Do you really want to ruin the vacation with the grandkids that we've planned for so long?"

He sighed and shuffled out of the cabin. She made a move to go after him, but stopped herself by reminding herself that if she followed it would just feed his victim behavior.

The next morning he avoided all eye contact with her. She knew he expected an apology from her because she had confronted him about his attitude. Instead of following her expected pattern, she asked, "Well, have you made your decision about going home?"

"What's gotten into you?" he deflected, insinuating that the problem did not arise from him but from her.

"Something that should have a long time ago. Seeing the grandkids brought down in the dumps by your sulking around just brought it home to me. I've suffered with it for a long time, but they aren't going to," she said flatly.

He looked baffled for a moment, as if he had lost his bearings. She got up and left the room.

He rushed to catch up with her.

"Every time you choose that behavior I feel like the man I love walked out the door and a different one walked in. One nobody really wants to spend time with. Do you like spending time with yourself when you're in that mood?"

He stopped and looked at her with a glimmer of understanding. "No. I don't like how I feel. But I don't think I can change it."

"People can change things about themselves when they really want to. We can both work on changing together. But right now that part of you that keeps you down and keeps the rest of us down with you—it needs to go. For the kids' sake, for me, but also for you."

You may say that Beverly's story sounds too easy, but that was just one example of her confronting Alan. It actually took her a lot longer to break herself from mothering him when he played the victim role. Nevertheless, the steps that she took are the same steps you should follow.

TAKE THESE STEPS

1. Look for consistency in his behavior as a victim.
2. Be alert to what emotions and maternal feelings come up for you.
3. Pay attention to how he gets you to defend him when no defense is necessary.
4. Detach your sympathy and a sense of responsibility when he plays his victim role.

Look for Consistency

By looking for consistency in the way he plays his victim role, you'll be better able to identify it as a way he gets you to spoil him. In other words, if he uses the victim role often and in a variety of ways, you can be more confident that his victim role is meant to manipulate you into taking care of him.

He may play the victim to encourage your sympathy and excuse his faults—he counts on your unwillingness to criticize a victim. In fact, he has a variety of ways to play victim. Here are some examples of behavior that should grab your attention. He can:

- Act easily wounded by you.
- Act stressed out so that you wouldn't dare confront him about anything.
- Be unable to laugh at himself.
- Complain about the endless number of people who have done him wrong.
- Complain about people who have done him an injustice.
- Act wounded and hurt by something someone said or did.

If you fall into the trap he's set for you, he'll get you to believe that you're his victimizer. Take this self-test:

1. Do you censor what you say to him because you fear that he will play victim?
2. Do you listen attentively and ask empathetic questions when he complains about an endless number of people who have done him wrong?
3. Do you apologize for hurting his feelings even though you did nothing offensive?

If you answered yes to just one of these questions, you're telling him that he is too fragile and needy to devote energy to paying attention to you. He thinks he's the center of the universe, and you're not only teaching him how to be spoiled but also that you don't matter.

Be Alert to Your Emotions

Is the CODE in place? Do you feel TRAPped? When he plays the victim, his aim is to stir up feelings in you such as:

- Sympathy
- Wanting to protect him
- Wanting to nurture him

By playing the victim, he distorts the relationship CODE. Instead of mutual **C**ompassion, it's all directed toward him. You don't feel **O**pen to bringing up his victim role because of how he'll react. The **D**epth of your relationship is lost because the focus is on his victimization. And finally, there's no **E**quality because you can't get attention for being a victim, too.

Like Beverly, many women don't catch on to how spoiled men can use the victim role until later in their relationship. In fact, most spoiled men who use the victim role aren't as obvious as Beverly's husband. You'll need to pay attention to your feelings, and I'm not referring to your maternal feelings, I'm referring to your feelings of frustration.

> YOU SHOULDN'T CONFUSE your maternal instincts with feeling responsible for him. He'll manipulate your compassion for him and turn you into his mother. Do you want a partner or a perpetually wounded child?

Because the victim role can be so effective, many women react by becoming emotionally frustrated and can't figure out what they are frustrated with. That's why you should pay close attention to whether or not you feel TRAPped. Ask yourself if you feel:

- **T**ense because you're always worried whether you're giving him enough support for being a victim or aware that he can play victim at any time

- **R**esentment because he let's you know that you're not giving him enough attention for his woes
- **A**ngry because he doesn't pay the same attention to you when you're a victim
- **P**owerless because you can't attend to your own needs while focusing on him

When he plays victim, it's hard to care for yourself. Like any good nurturer, you set aside your own needs to care for a victim. Since you know that you're not a victim and assume that he is, you think that you can get back to your needs after caring for his. The problem is, this assumption is *wrong*. He's not a temporary victim; it's a permanent role that he plays.

> HAVE YOU EVER wondered what exactly attracted him to you? Was it your looks or maybe your personality? If you guessed it was your caring nature or your compassion, you're probably right. He found you, a person who is comfortable taking care of others, exactly the kind of person he needs.

Of course he needs situations to play off as they come up. He probably milks each incident for all he can get out of it. As soon as he senses that your sympathy is fading, he'll distort another situation to make him look like a victim.

Pay Attention: Are You Defending Him?

When he plays the victim, you may feel compelled to defend him to family and friends who are critical of him. When they try to get you to look at how you're spoiling him, you may still defend him. When they express their concerns for you and criticize him, you might find yourself saying, "Can't you give him a break?"

IT'S NATURAL FOR mothers to nurture and protect their children, provide sympathy, and sometimes excuse immature behavior. A spoiled man never stops needing this coddling. Why should a grown woman feel compelled to treat a grown man like a child? You're going to have to push him out of the crib.

Detach Your Sympathy

Now that you have a better understanding of how he uses the victim role to get you to spoil him, let's focus on what you can do to avoid being manipulated by it. The first step is to detach yourself from any responsibility to protect him or obligation to have sympathy for his role of victim.

The key here is to focus on the fact that it is a role that he is playing. If he says that he feels victimized by someone who really isn't guilty of the offense, you should resist the pull to align yourself with him against that person. The less support you give to his role, the better.

This effort to detach your sympathy must be done in a neutral and even an astonished manner. In other words, just as you should not support his victim role so too is it unwise to be openly critical of him for it. It's wiser to express your astonishment that he thinks he's a victim. Your true sympathy can come in if you feel sorry for him because he thinks of himself as a victim, not because he is a victim.

REAL-LIFE EXAMPLE

Let's say you're out to dinner with another couple. For the most part, you're having a good time. All of a sudden, your partner gives you a nasty look. You look surprised, as if to question his look. But you know that he took offense when you mentioned that he almost ran out of gas on the way to the restaurant.

After saying goodbye to the other couple, he begins the silent treatment. Out of habit, you're tempted to ask him what's wrong. But you know that if you do you'll keep yourself on the losing end. So you bite your lip and the tense silence continues. When it's clear you're not going to say anything, he says, "Thanks" in a sarcastic tone.

"For what, honey?" you ask with a nurturing tone, making your question more of a comment.

"What do you mean, for what? You didn't have to call me irresponsible!"

"When did I do that?" you ask with a reflective question.

"Almost ran out of gas? Are you calling me careless?"

You look at him sympathetically and say, "Wow! You're on edge. Are you feeling okay?"

If he still goes on, don't give up any ground.

Here's another example. Let's say your spoiled man is intimidated by your intellect. If he responds to your intellectual curiosity by playing victim, he's asking you to spoil him. He might feel inferior and try to imply that you're arrogant or showing off.

Use a nurturing comment followed by a way to escape the conversation. Say something like "Oh, I'm sorry. I thought you were interested in the subject." He might say that he was interested but that he didn't get a chance to say anything.

Respond by saying, "I'd love to get your opinion on it."

Then he'll probably say something like "You've already touched on the main points."

At that point say, "Well, I'm open to hear about the main points as you see them."

WHY DOES *The Victim* always seem to need sympathy? Maybe he grew up confusing the feelings of love and sympathy. You can help him to finally free himself of this crippling role by being sympathetic only when it is truly warranted. And, most importantly, you can free yourself of the burden of mothering him.

EXAMPLES OF MEN WHO PLAY VICTIMS

Some spoiled men have a knack for playing the burdened one when they are actually doing the burdening. A Passive Pete once complained to me that his wife was frustrated with him because he made little effort to work full-time. She also called him passive-aggressive. Asked what he was doing to meet her expectations, he responded by saying, "She knew my lifestyle before we started living together. Now she expects me to change." He went on to complain that she didn't understand and asked, "Why can't she give me a break?"

Another spoiled man complained that a series of women broke up with him because "they didn't understand that need to live out my dream of being an artist." The fact was he didn't sell enough art to support himself and he wanted his various girlfriends to help support him.

Always playing the victim, he had little insight into the fact that he was the subtle victimizer. Part of the reason why he had a hard time understanding how he was to blame was that he did nothing overt to cause any pain. His victimizing was more like water torture. There was the drip, drip, drip of his passive going-less-than-halfway behavior, causing each woman in his life to finally give up on him. He had them fooled for a while because he was very good at acting warm and concerned about them.

> *THE VICTIM* IS WHINEY. He learned along the way to adulthood that in order to get warmth and attention he had to arouse sympathy in others. Maybe you're tired of hearing it or maybe you feel sorry for him. Whatever the reason, it's not your responsibility to soothe his never-ending "hurt" feelings, nor is it good for him.

Another spoiled man turned down an offer for a full-time position because his wife had just quit her job. A truly warm and concerned man would have responded to her resignation as a reason to pick up the slack and accept the offer for a full-time job. Instead, he played victim and an unequal partner by saying "How can she quit and put the burden on me to be the full-time employee?"

Accusing her of forcing him to work full-time got him back in the victim role again, right where he wanted to be. He hoped that making her feel guilty or sorry for him would prompt her to provide what he thought he needed—her going back to work so that he would be off the hook.

> *THE VICTIM* IS THE walking-wounded, silently-suffering type. But how much of the time is he truly suffering? Is he just acting like he's in pain in order to get his needs met? Unfortunately, until he matures and rejects his victim role, he will punish you for seeing through him. This won't be pleasant, but it won't last a lifetime. Remember, if you don't challenge the victim role, he will play it for life—and what kind of life will that be for you?

SUMMING UP THE VICTIM

By assuming the role of victim, a spoiled man taps into your compassion and gets you to protect and care for him. Because this works so well, whenever he sees the opportunity, he'll position himself in his victim role to gain power over you.

Your plan should be to see through the façade of his role as victim. Withdraw your sympathy when he is playing the part. Act astonished when he explains how he is the victim in a situation where he clearly is not, then tell him in a neutral voice that you don't understand. Turn his method of victimization around so that he traps himself into revealing that he is merely playing the role of victim.

CHAPTER 4

checkup quiz
Challenging the Victim

1. If he tells you that he has been victimized by numerous people throughout his life:
   a. You should do what you can to protect him from the cruel world.
   b. Look for a pattern, and if he turns normal situations into rationalizations for being a victim, withdraw your sympathy.
   c. Soothe his hurt feelings to make up for what others did to him.
   d. Make sure that he doesn't think you victimize him, too.

2. If he plays victim in a situation where you know that he's not a victim:
   a. Chalk it up to him being overly sensitive.
   b. Help him justify his victim role if the other person denies it.
   c. Tell him the truth if asked your opinion.
   d. Agree with him when he asks you your opinion, because if you don't he'll feel even more hurt.

3. If he blames you for something you didn't do:
   a. Tell him you're sorry so that you can move on.
   b. Tell him clearly and in a neutral voice that you didn't do it, nor do you want to spend more time talking about it.
   c. Bite your tongue and hope that he will forget about it.
   d. Consider the possibility that you victimized him in a way that you don't recognize.

4. When he fails at some task that you expected him to perform and blames another for making him fail:
   a. Find that person and let him have a piece of your mind.
   b. Hold him responsible and ask him to do it again the next time it needs to be done.
   c. Excuse him from the expectation because he did make the effort.
   d. Confirm his story with the person he says made him fail.

5. When he acts wounded by what another person said, yet you fail to see that it's offensive:
   a. Get the person to apologize.
   b. Don't buy into his victimization—focus on something constructive.
   c. Look for hidden meaning in what the person said.
   d. Agree with him that the other person was rude and needs to be punished for her cruelty.

6. When he describes in great detail how another person has victimized him but it's evident that it didn't happen:
   a. Sympathize with him so that he will feel better and move on to something else.
   b. Ask for more details until he convinces you.
   c. Gently point out the illogic in his story.
   d. Tell him that he was victimized because the other person was jealous of him.

7. If he plays victim when he is actually the victimizer:
   a. Agree with him so that he won't victimize you.
   b. Support his justification for being angry and getting back at the other person.
   c. When asked for your support, tell him that you will support his effort to make it right with the other person.
   d. Tell him that the other person needs to repent.

8. When he winces at something you said that you know was not hurtful:
   a. Apologize profusely and tell him that you would never say that again.
   b. Ask him for clarification as to what he was reacting to.
   c. Stay away from that subject and anything else remotely related to it.
   d. Try to cheer him up to make it up to him.

9. If he avoids a mutual friend who he unjustly feels victimized him:
   a. Tell that friend that your friendship with him is over.
   b. Secretly avoid that friend and don't tell him why.
   c. Carry on with the friendship and be available to coherently talk through any difficulties with your friend.
   d. Get your other mutual friends to blackball the supposed victimizer.

10. If he shuns or treats coldly someone who intimidates him:
    a. Shun her, too.
    b. Come up with reasons why that person is flawed.
    c. Carry on with that person as if you aren't intimidated.
    d. Defend him against the other person even if there is nothing to defend against.

5

Sheltering from the Emotional Storm

We all experience changes in our moods. For most of us, those changes are not extreme, and we generally try to keep them from bothering those around us. It's not easy to be around someone who is in a bad mood and tries to make us feel responsible for it. You may have heard the saying, "He coughs and you catch the flu." A spoiled man wants his emotional climate to dominate, so when he's down in the dumps, he wants you to be down too.

However, he may even go one step further and blame you for his rotten mood. The danger is that because of his behavior, his moods can become your moods. Your task should be to shelter yourself from a spoiled man's moods by learning how to detach from his emotional storm and let him stew in his own self-pity.

THE LOCAL HARDWARE store would do a booming business selling an "emotional barometer." If it worked, it would offer a valuable service to every place of employment and every home!

In the following story, Beth struggles to stay emotionally healthy when in the company of her moody husband. Notice how she learned to shift the responsibility for his moods back to him rather than allowing him to place the blame on her. She was able to accomplish this by making a statement with her behavior that he would not be able to derail her plans.

STEVE AND BETH

Beth told me that she often felt emotionally fatigued after spending long periods of time with her husband, Steve. This was because she spent so much energy protecting him from being hurt all the time. After four years of marriage, she learned that if she could take a break from what they were doing together and engage in something else alone that emotionally refueled her, she could come back and finish what they were doing together.

Steve was an expert at getting Beth to carry the conversation for both of them. If he didn't like what they were talking about, he would grow sullen and say something like, "Can't we talk about something else?" But he would never suggest what that something else might be.

Sometimes when they'd drive together, he would grow quiet. Beth became convinced that he was waiting for her to pull him out of an abyss. She would search for something to say while he'd sit with a sour face or turn away with a grimace. It seemed less a question of the topic and more a matter of lifting his never-buoyant moods. Though I never met him, her description of his behavior made me wonder if he was dysthymic, meaning mildly depressed. I encouraged her to ask him to seek help. According to her, he flatly rejected the idea.

Beth's Own Emotions

Regarding her own emotions, she would rarely tell him if she was sad or disappointed about something that had happened to

her during the day. When she did tell him, after a few obliga-
tory condolences, she would feel him getting depressed. She
knew that, to him, it was her job to abandon her own feelings
and take care of his.

While Beth made the decisions in their lives, Steve was reac-
tive and never failed to let her know that what she had arranged
wasn't good enough. Even when things went fine, he wouldn't
acknowledge that her decisions had worked out well.

Usually she would have to talk him into doing something
fun. He would think of a hundred reasons why it wasn't a good
idea before saying, "Well, if you really want to. I guess."

Beth's Confrontation

One day after our third session she spent an hour trying
to talk him into going to the mountains for a hike. He finally
replied, "All right, already. I'll go if you get off my back."

She almost changed her mind about inviting him, believing
that he would bring his emotional dark clouds up to the mountains and make it a miserable trip. She looked him over for a
moment while remembering from our sessions that she needed
to make a paradoxical comment. "You're right. You wouldn't
have a good time up there."

"How do you know that?" he responded.

Then she remembered that I suggested she make her next
comment nurturing. "It sounds like you're not in the mood.
Maybe you ought to stay here and take care of yourself."

"What are you going to do?"

"Go to the mountains, of course," she said, and started to
pack a lunch for herself.

"What? You're going to leave me here?"

"I don't want to put you through the agonizing experience of
driving up into the mountains when you don't feel like it."

"Why don't you let me be the judge of that?"

"Good idea. I feel very uncomfortable being put into the

position of making decisions for you," she said, then left the room with her bag.

He followed her into the garage. "Can't you wait? I'm coming."

"Only if you really want to."

"Why would I come if I don't want to?" he asked as he stuffed some snacks into his daypack.

"That's a good question. Maybe you have the answer to that."

On the drive up to the mountains he didn't provide the answer. He drove silently, waiting for her to provide the conversation.

She decided that she would break new ground and match his silence with her own. She put on some music. He said, "You really like this music?"

She glanced at him then plugged in earphones for herself. After an hour of listening to her music, she told him to drive into the dirt parking lot marked by a sign "Castle Peak Trailhead."

"You really want to hike here?" he asked in a disappointed voice.

"That's right," she said, getting out of the car. "I'll meet you here in three hours. Go where you want."

"I thought we were going to hike together."

"As I said, only if you want to, and it doesn't sound like you do."

"I said I'll go, since you're making such a big deal about it," he said in a sad tone.

She looked at him. "You truly can't hear yourself, can you? Listen, it's a nice sunny day and I don't want you dragging dark clouds along. So meet me here in three hours." She shut the door and hiked up the trail.

For the first ten minutes of the hike she debated turning back, feeling that she had been too harsh and blunt. Gradually, the crisp mountain air cleared up that guilt. Then she came to a meadow with an open view of Castle Peak and was delighted to be alone at that moment.

As she hiked back to the parking lot three hours later, she tried to develop a plan to deal with his sulkiness. The car was in the lot but he wasn't in it. As she walked up to the car, she realized that she didn't have the key.

He cleared his throat. She glanced over to the trees where he sat with a glum face.

"So, did you enjoy your time?"

"What do you think?" he said in a sarcastic tone.

"Thanks. You confirmed that I made a good decision to hike alone. No dark clouds on my hike."

He mumbled something to himself as he stood up. In the past she would have asked him what he said. She decided she already had a pretty good hunch and didn't want to bathe in his gloom with him.

The drive back began with more grumpy silent treatment. She grabbed her earphones.

"I'll listen to your music," he said.

"Only if you want to," she said, glancing at him. At his nod, she popped the CD into the player.

Within a minute, he said, "Could you turn it down?"

She knew that he could have turned it down himself and she didn't want to listen to the music with a wet blanket smothering it. So she put the earphones back on. She kept her eyes on the road ahead. A glance his way would give him an opportunity to punish her. Also, she didn't bother to try conversation with him at home that night because his silent treatment grew a sharp edge. He closed doors and cabinets with more force than was necessary to punctuate his displeasure with her independence.

Beth's Persistence

At dinner the next evening, she made sure not to be responsible for the conversation. But she was ready to participate in it if he managed to be pleasant. He didn't try. Finally, he said, "What's got into you?"

"I'm just learning to take care of myself."

"What the hell does that mean?"

"I'm learning to resist allowing your moods to control things."

It took Beth a sustained effort for a few months before Steve got the clear message that his moods were his responsibility. She would no longer spoil him because of his moods. Just as I taught Beth, you need to take these steps to immunize yourself from his moods.

TAKE THESE STEPS

1. Don't change your behavior because of his moods.
2. When he tries to make you responsible for his moods, reject that responsibility.
3. Distance yourself from his moods.
4. Let his moods backfire on him.
5. Shift your focus onto something that you can enjoy by yourself and do not allow him to join you and bring you down.

Before you try to take these steps, it will be helpful to understand how he manipulates you. Like Steve, your man wants you to take care of him emotionally, but when he's cranky, moody, and sullen you must deal with the emotional fallout. He controls the emotional climate of your relationship by:

- Trying to make you feel guilty for his bad mood, as if you caused it
- Throwing out cranky comments and being irritable
- Sulking
- Brooding
- Complaining
- Whining

All of these techniques encourage you to spoil him by getting you to:

- Feel responsible for his moods.
- Cheer him up.
- "Go easy" on him because he's already "in a mood."
- Center your attention on him.

You may think that if you could change his mood, neither of you would have to suffer. Over time both of you adjust to your efforts to make his bad moods go away. He does less to control them and you do more to try to control them. What a deal for him! His moods have become your responsibility.

HAS *MOODY* SAID, "I can't control how I feel"? Don't fall for that nonsense! Chances are that he can control how he feels, he just doesn't want to take that responsibility. Wouldn't you rather only be responsible for one person's mood—your own?

Don't Change Your Behavior

He's off the hook from having to do what most adults must do—namely, be responsible for balancing his own moods. Unfortunately for you, he's got you to try to balance his moods for him. This leaves you with the task of balancing yours and his at the same time.

Over time, you increasingly make adjustments to accommodate his bad moods. You dare not throw bad moods back to him, because he's already in a bad mood and throwing it back to him will get him in a worse mood.

EVERYONE EXPERIENCES a bad mood now and then, but the *Moody* spoiled man specializes in them. So, don't you specialize in being a trash can for his bad moods. He doesn't have PMS!

He wants you to adjust to his moodiness. It's on his agenda for you to change whatever you are doing to take care of him, but it's in your best interest to stay with your own plans and not change your behavior. Just as Beth went for a hike in the mountains despite Steve's grumpiness, you too should follow through with your plans.

Reject Responsibility for His Moods

Your challenge is to find shelter from his bad moods without owning any responsibility for them. To accomplish this seemingly impossible task, you've got to learn to recognize how he sucks you into his emotional storms. He does this by:

- The tone of his voice
- Angry glares
- Downcast eyes
- Shaking his head after something you said
- Becoming quiet and sullen
- Depressed and irritable body language, such as sunken shoulders

It's hard to keep from feeling sorry for him because you've learned to respond to all these techniques as if they are cues to prompt you into your caretaking role. As soon as you start trying to make him feel better, he'll make you try harder.

Distance Yourself from His Moods

Recognize his moods as tools that he uses to manipulate you into spoiling him. Just as Steve successfully manipulated Beth into taking care of his moods, your spoiled man can do it to you, too. And just as Beth learned to untangle herself from his moods and see them for what they were (methods of manipulation), you can also distance yourself from his moods.

HE COULD BE playing on your maternal instinct to care for and soothe him. Don't forget, though, even if he was your little boy you wouldn't want to reward sulkiness with attention.

His dark emotional clouds hang over the CODE of your relationship. It's hard for you to have Compassion for him when he is weighing you down with his heavy wet blanket of bad moods. And certainly he demonstrates little compassion for you in the process. It's hard to be Open when he turns everything into a negative. You don't want to Deepen the relationship for fear of getting into even more depressing territory. Finally, there is little Equality in a relationship dominated by his emotional storms. From his point of view, your moods don't equal his in importance.

Let His Moods Backfire

It's time to change the rules. You should let him suffer the consequences of his moodiness. He won't be able to suffer those consequences and deal with his own emotions if you try to fix them for him. You need to step away from being tangled up in his emotions.

YOU CAN'T MAKE his bad moods go away. If you try to, he'll keep dumping them on you. That's one present that you never want to be given. Pay attention to your own needs and what it will take to keep your own spirit lifted.

When you walk up to quicksand, a sidestep will save you from sinking. If you miss that sidestep and end up in the quicksand, expecting to swim out is a losing proposition. Getting stuck taking care of his moods is the same thing; you end up feeling TRAPped. Pay attention to those TRAPped feelings by asking yourself if you:

- Feel tense around him because you never know what mood he's going to be in.
- Resent him bringing you down all the time.
- Feel angry because he can express his anger but you have to repress yours.
- Feel powerless around him because his moods dominate.

Rechannel those feelings into changing the way you react to his moods.

Shift Your Focus

To detach from his emotional storms, you'll need something else to focus on. Find something that will fully engage your attention, such as a hobby or a club. And make sure that he can't participate in it. This is important because if you allow him to participate in it, he'll drag you down in the same emotional quicksand. Thus, changing what you're doing and including him in it only defeats the purpose. It would be as if you'd painted yourself into a corner with him in that tight space with you.

Remember how Beth dealt with Steve's comment about the music in the car? She wanted to hear the CD at a reasonable volume and knew that she needed to focus on something other than his manipulations. So she decided to put earphones on and to focus on the music without him.

BODY LANGUAGE AND TONE OF VOICE

A spoiled man can get to you not only by what he says but also by the tone of his voice. A downbeat tone can color a positive statement black. This tone is meant to cue you to prop up his mood. If you fail at your assignment, he may add sad body language. At this point you might feel compelled to ask him if he is okay.

Since it's probably his usual manipulation, you need to come up with a new strategy. If he attempts to pull you in using the tone of his voice and body language, try responding to the content of what he says. If he colors the content of what he says with sarcasm or even gloominess, it's time to change the subject. In the following story, notice how shifting a spoiled man's attention can help you to avoid spoiling him.

Catherine and Bob

One morning Catherine was sitting on the patio gazing out at the green rolling hills of Northern California. Her husband, Bob, came out to join her. Within less than a minute he directed her attention to a house a mile away atop a hill. This house was recently built and had no trees planted around it.

"That house really spoils everything," he said.

"Yes, there ought to be a law against that!" she quickly said.

Though she was a proponent of building ordinances that prevent ridgetop houses, she didn't want to be brought down by thinking about it at that moment when there was the spectacular view and springtime flowers to enjoy. The house was a mere speck in the distance and it seemed the actual house was not the issue, he just happened to be in a bad mood and wanted to share it.

There was no fighting him, she thought. Even her attempt to redirect his attention to a hawk that flew by didn't work. He continued to lament the house off in the distance, missing everything else. She remembered what we had talked about in our counseling sessions, so she stopped trying to help him focus on something else. Instead, she focused on what she wanted to accomplish that morning. But he continued to go on and on about the house on the hill.

She looked at him with an astonished expression and said, "Is that house all you see this morning?"

"Uh . . . no . . . but . . ."

"Great, what else do you see?"

"Well, the colors in the flowers."

By inviting him to tell her about positive things around the house she was able to shift his attention and let him know that she would not listen to his negative comments.

SUMMING UP EMOTIONAL STORMS

One of the ways he gets you to spoil him is by letting his moods throw you off-balance. His moodiness can be oppressive, so you do whatever you can to keep him in a good mood. Heaven forbid that you upset him! Then, however, you pay, not only by having to be around him when he is down, sulky, irritable, or angry but also by being blamed for his moodiness.

Your plan should be to let his moodiness be his responsibility. Distance yourself from him when he is moody or trying to punish you with one of his emotional storms. If he tries to punish you for his moods, let those moods backfire on him so that he must stew in them by himself.

CHAPTER 5

checkup quiz
Sheltering from the Emotional Storm

1. If his moods control the emotional climate of the household:
   a. Get a weather report each morning to find out how your day will go.
   b. Try to soothe him so that he will have fewer bad moods.
   c. During his bad moods, tell him how much you appreciate him.
   d. Show him that you can't be controlled by his moods by maintaining a good mood when he's in a bad one and avoiding him when necessary.

2. If he blames you for his bad mood, you should:
   a. Ask him what you did so that you won't do it again.
   b. Do your best to cheer him up.
   c. Let him know in as neutral a tone as possible that his moods are his responsibility.
   d. Keep your mouth shut so that you won't upset him even more.

3. If he is irritable with you and it seems that there is nothing you can do right:
   a. Keep your distance to insure that he can't use you as a trash can for his moods.
   b. Try harder, because sooner or later you will calm him down.
   c. Ask him to have mercy on you.
   d. Consider the possibility that you can't do anything right.

4. When he sits in silence stewing in a bad mood, you:
   a. Ask him if there's something you did to put him in a bad mood.
   b. Pretend that he isn't in a bad mood and chatter on about your day.
   c. Search for a subject that will grab his attention.
   d. Focus on something that will grab your attention.

5. During his periods of positive moods:
   a. Show him attention and note that you enjoy his company.
   b. Grit your teeth because sooner or later he'll slip into a bad mood.
   c. Wonder if he's trying to butter you up for something.
   d. Praise him for having a good mood.

6. When he comes home from work in a bad mood:
   a. Do what you can to get him out of it.
   b. Make sure that whatever responsibilities he had (such as doing the dishes) he is relieved of.
   c. Offer to talk through whatever happened. If he rejects your offer avoid him until he gets himself out of the bad mood.
   d. Pretend that he isn't in a bad mood.

7. When he sulks after something both of you find disappointing happened:
   a. Put aside your disappointment to try to get him to look at the silver lining.
   b. Compete with him to see who can be more disappointed.
   c. Tell him that you weren't disappointed and try to convince him not to feel that way, either.
   d. Work on trying to make the best of it for yourself.

8. If he seems to be down and waits for you to cheer him up:
   a. Plan his day so that he will encounter few problems.
   b. Tell him as many jokes as possible.
   c. Ask him if he is happy with you.
   d. Restrain your impulse to cheer him up and work toward developing plans for your own day.

9. If he gets angry with you for something you didn't do:
   a. Make up for both of you.
   b. Try to make things better by being cheerful and pretend nothing happened.
   c. Remain clear, firm, and civil about his need to apologize.
   d. Get quiet until his emotional storm blows over.

10. If you go on a day trip together and he is in a stinking mood:
    a. Ask him if he wants to change the plans because you interpret his mood to suggest that he doesn't like the plans you developed.
    b. Pretend that he's not in a bad mood and chatter about the landscape as you drive.
    c. Ask him if he would like to be dropped off at home because he doesn't seem to be feeling well.
    d. Assume that he's angry at you for something, so be nice in the hope that he'll sooner or later tell you what it is.

6

Remaining Optimistic with a Pessimist

A spoiled man often demands that you be the optimist for both of you while he plays the pessimist. This can be emotionally exhausting for you, while being pessimistic is easy for him because you're there to offer encouragement or suggestions to look on the bright side. In this chapter, you'll learn how to remain optimistic about your own life and not be brought down by his pessimism.

Dealing with a spoiled man's pessimism is similar in many ways to dealing with his moodiness. But it's more complicated because it has to do with how the two of you approach the future, not just everyday moods.

It's easy to come up with reasons why something might not work out perfectly. That's because there is no such thing as a perfect situation. A spoiled man will remind you of that constantly. When he reminds you that things aren't perfect, you may feel compelled to make up the difference. Since he's unwilling to do it, he asks you to do it for him, but doesn't come right out and ask directly.

He uses various tricks to get you to do it, including:

- Acting disappointed that things aren't working out the way he had hoped
- Complaining that there are negative possibilities in any given situation
- Subtly blaming you for failing to come up with a plan or ideas that are perfect
- Coming up with myriad reasons why something won't work out

For example, if you tell him there's one piece of cake left, he complains that it's a smaller piece than yours—which gets you to trade plates. Or you might tell him you had the car cleaned and he'll complain that they probably used stinky air freshener.

Whatever the scenario, his pessimism manifests, and he gets you to overcompensate and use up your mental energy to try to show Mr. Sourpuss that it's not as bad as he thinks it is. Consider the story of Sunny and Todd.

TODD AND SUNNY

Sunny came in for counseling soon after meeting Todd. She didn't know if she wanted to go out with him again because he seemed so pessimistic about life. She decided to say yes to another date but had some regrets.

She told me that she met Todd at a mutual friend's wedding. During the reception they found themselves at the same table. "So, what do you do?" Todd asked.

"I'm a nurse," Sunny said.

"Oh, that must be really hard being with all those ill people."

"Not really. I find it fulfilling to help people."

Todd looked unconvinced. "You sure that's not a bunch of happy talk?"

"Shouldn't we be positive about what we do? How 'bout you?"

"I'm dreading going back to work on Monday. That answer your question?" he said with downcast eyes.

"What do you do?"

"Tech support," he said. "Everyone wants their computer fixed yesterday."

"I guess people are already frustrated by the time they get to you for help. You could help them feel more at ease."

"I'm not a therapist or nurse," he said flatly.

Missed Red Flags

Sunny left the reception with mixed feelings. While she was quite attracted to Todd, he left her with a lingering feeling of discomfort. During the reception two friends had nodded their approval of her sitting with Todd. Yet as she drove home she felt strangely saddened.

Todd called her two days later to ask her out on a date. Before she answered she asked how he was doing at work.

"Oh, it's Monday."

"I guess Monday can be good too," she said, trying to be positive.

"Right," he said, as if he thought she was joking. "Anyway, do you want to go out?"

She wasn't quite sure. When he mentioned the movie he had chosen she decided that she would go because she had been wanting to see it.

When he picked her up for the date on Friday she asked, "So how is everything going?"

"TGIF, you know."

She shrugged her shoulders and hopped into the car thinking that it may be a good idea to change the subject. "I'm really looking forward to seeing the movie."

"Probably a lot of other people are, too. I hope it's not sold out."

When they pulled into the theater parking lot they noticed the long line in front of the ticket booth.

"Oh boy. I was afraid of that. I hope we'll get in before the movie starts."

"If we don't, there's always a different movie or another night," she said, then wondered if she wanted to commit herself to another evening together. She was just getting to know him.

On the drive home he noted that his car was "on its last leg."

"Oh really," she said. "It looks new to me."

"Well, you know these all-wheel-drives," he said with a sarcastic tone.

She wanted to ask why he bought that type of car if he was less than confident in its longevity. Instead, she said, "I bet it's useful in the snow."

"If this drought will ever break there would be some skiing up there."

"Great. You ski?"

"Do you want to go sometime?"

She nodded yes. "If there's enough snow."

Todd shrugged his shoulders. "Next weekend?"

We had our next counseling session before the ski trip. I suggested that she use any opportunity that he presented to her to show him that his pessimism wouldn't change her plans nor induce her to waste energy trying to get him to share her optimism.

The ride up to the mountains was frustrating, but Sunny tried to make the best of it.

"I wish this rain would turn to snow," Todd said as they drove up into the foothills.

"Wait till we get to the higher elevations when it gets colder," she said, then regretted taking his bait and playing the optimist. It was time to shift out of that role before he expects it from her. "Then again, it may not."

"We'll see," Todd said.

As Sunny had predicted, it began to snow as they rose in elevation.

"Still looks like wet snow," he said in a concerned voice.

She almost found herself justifying it, but she caught herself and instead just said, "Yup."

Under blue skies during lunch, Sunny said, "Couldn't ask for better weather."

He pointed to a cloud on the horizon.

Resisting His Pessimism

Sunny found herself composing an upbeat response but decided that it was time to shift to a different track. She knew that she didn't want to constantly tell him that everything was going to be okay. She also wanted to make sure that she didn't descend into a pessimistic attitude with him. It was time for her to show him that his pessimism was not going to rule her day.

At the end of their day of skiing he asked, "Want to catch dinner before we brave that miserable traffic?"

"I'll drive if you like," she said.

"I'd still be a passenger."

She took a long sympathetic look at him. "Yeah, that might be hard for you."

Todd looked embarrassed but not offended, because Sunny expressed sympathy for him. The piggyback message that he alone would be bothered by the traffic came in under the radar screen. "I'll drive," he said in a disappointed voice.

On the way down the crowded mountain road, Todd sighed loudly and squirmed in the driver's seat. Sunny knew a pessimistic comment was on the way. She too was getting uncomfortable with the traffic but she didn't want to hear about his frustration. "Could you get off on this off-ramp? I need to use the bathroom."

"Sure, but the traffic will get thicker," he said matter-of-factly.

His insensitive response to her need to use the bathroom especially irked her. It told her that his pessimism was the most important driving force so early in their relationship.

As she walked up to the car after going to the restroom she said, "There's a restaurant over there. Let's catch some dinner."

"Do you think it's a good restaurant?" he asked in a pessimistic tone.

"I have no idea. If you have any better ideas, I'm open."

"Well, I don't know, the options are slim now."

"Which one of the slim options do you want to take?"

He shook his head as if to say that he didn't have any ideas that he felt positive about. "I guess we can go over there if you want."

Sunny was feeling set up. She didn't want to be held accountable if the restaurant did not meet his expectations. "If you think the restaurant won't be that good, I'm fine with driving on."

He reflected for a moment. "We better get something to eat."

Sunny actually did continue to see Todd, though not as frequently as he wanted. Eventually, she managed to box him into making positive statements because she refused to do it for him. As he became more of an optimist she found him more enjoyable to be around.

Whatever the stage of your relationship, you can restructure your relationship with a pessimistic man. This structure must include clear steps.

TAKE THESE STEPS

1. Resist the impulse to convince him that his pessimism should be replaced with your optimism.
2. Decide that his pessimism is his responsibility.
3. Step back and allow him the space to learn how to develop optimism.
4. Cultivate optimism within yourself and in your actions.

THE LIFE OF *The Pessimist* is sad. You probably feel a lot of sympathy for him. You may feel like giving him a hug and telling him that everything is going to be okay. Don't do it! The problem is that if you do, it will only make him worse.

Resist Replacing His Pessimism with Your Optimism

Because a spoiled man can use pessimism as a way of controlling you, it's difficult to avoid being manipulated by his negativism. Not only does he ask you to get him to look on the bright side, but he wears you out with his downbeat view of the world. He wants you to:

- Work hard so that all the imperfections are swept out of his way.
- Try to persuade him that everything is going okay.
- Keep coming up with ideas and plans that will be perfect despite his constant complaints that they may not work out.
- Feel guilty for not arranging for a better outcome.

All of these tactics put you on notice to try as hard as you can to prove to him that his pessimism is unwarranted. Ironically, the harder you try the more he digs in, resisting your efforts.

HOW MANY TIMES a week do you try to get him to look on the bright side? It's like being a cheerleader for an eternally glum team. There's a better way to support him: step out of your usual role as cheerleader and let him learn how to cheer himself up.

Make His Pessimism His Responsibility

A pessimistic spoiled man challenges everything you offer with a "yes, but." This puts you in the position of trying to talk him into thinking on the bright side. It's as if you're being asked to drag him into the positive future that he is unwilling to help create.

Step Back: Allow Him to Develop Optimism

Optimism is one of the most important characteristics of emotional intelligence. Pessimism paints him into a depressing emotional corner. People who are generally pessimistic tend to cultivate a depressing view of the world. People who are optimistic tend not to, and generally enjoy their lives more because of their optimism. By stepping back from the responsibility of being his optimist, you allow him the opportunity to develop that skill for himself.

Cultivate Optimism Within Yourself

If you are perpetually stuck being the optimistic part of the relationship, he's got you where he wants you. What a deal for him! He doesn't need to come up with any ideas; he can sit back and complain about yours. At any step along the way he can play the pessimist to try to get you to work harder to make things right. Your job is to hold onto optimism for yourself. When you pull back from being his optimist, reinvest your energy into cultivating an optimistic attitude for yourself.

REAL-LIFE EXAMPLE

Let's say you suggest going to the beach with your partner. He says, "Oh, I don't know. It might be foggy."

After checking the weather report you say, "No, the forecast say's it's going to be clear."

"Probably because it's windy," he says.

"It didn't say anything about wind," you counter.

"You know the weatherman," he says with sarcasm.

"True, but we can always leave if it gets windy."

"Then what would be the point of going?"

What he's really saying is, "Drag me out there, and I reserve the right to complain on the way there and back."

So, let's say you take his bait and do "drag" him out there. Let's also say that it's not foggy or windy. You begin to enjoy yourself and hope that he will, too. But five minutes later he complains, "There may be too many people coming here today."

"Yeah, they're all taking advantage of the great weather," you say, but you've had enough doom and gloom by now.

In this situation, you would do well to hand him the car keys and say, "I'm sorry this has been so hard for you. Go ahead and drive back home." This will serve to knock him off-balance. Give in to what he says the problem is rather than cater to his mood.

He may be so flabbergasted by your willingness to do something extreme to escape his pessimism that he tries to stall by asking, "So how are you going to get back home?"

"I see the Baker family over there. I'll get a ride home with them."

As the optimist in the relationship, your job is to assure him that you'll foresee having a good time despite his pessimism. Affirm that you're only saving him from himself by saying something like "I don't want to put you through this misery while I'm having a good time."

"I was only making conversation."

"And do you think I want to hear your worrying about the number of people coming here?" you say in as neutral a tone as possible.

"Well, I'm sorry," he snaps.

"Apology accepted."

He looks at a loss for words. As he stares at you expecting you to salvage the situation, you say, "I'll see you at home."

"Wait!" he says as you begin to walk away. "I'm staying."

"With that pessimistic attitude?"

"I said I was sorry."

"But I don't want you to have a bad time."

"I won't."

"Okay, I'll give you a chance to prove it."

Now you have him in a bind. He's got to act like he's enjoying himself to prove it. Otherwise you can present the car keys again as a paradoxical way to be nurturing.

The bottom line is that if you look hard enough at anything you'll find flaws. It's coming up with solutions and being willing to stand up and be counted for trying that is important.

> WHY DOES *The Pessimist* seem so downbeat about everything? Could it be learned behavior modeled by family members? Maybe he has learned that by thinking things will turn out poorly, when they do he is not disappointed. You can make yourself sick trying to figure that one out. Whatever his reason, it's not your responsibility to coddle him like he's a sad child.

APPLYING THE CODE

A spoiled man's pessimism wears down the CODE of your relationship. While you offer Compassion to him in an effort to alleviate his pessimism, he offers none in return. You don't feel Open to discuss your frustration with him because of his pessimism. He'll make you pay by saying something pessimistic about your relationship. Optimism does offer Depth via possibilities, but his pessimism shuts things down into a shallow relationship. The imbalance between his pessimism and your optimism defeats Equality.

If you accept his ploy to get you to explain how things are okay, you put yourself in a no-win situation. It's an impossible task because he'll come up with endless reasons why you're wrong. This only makes you try harder.

> TO BE RESPONSIBLE for elevating the outlook of another person *all* of the time is draining. You will feel like a big sponge that is constantly being squeezed dry. Once you've become a dried-up sponge, you may resort to becoming a pessimist just like him—and then where will you both be, with no one to bring either of you out of it?

As you run yourself into the ground trying to do the impossible, you'll become emotionally exhausted.

TRAPPED FEELINGS

Pay close attention to the feelings of being TRAPped. Ask yourself if you feel:

- Tense because you anticipate his pessimism about anything you plan
- Resentment because despite your efforts, he still finds reasons why things won't work out
- Anger because as you try to enjoy yourself he casts a negative prediction that the experience will turn bad
- Powerless because no matter what you say, he digs in his heels and stays negative

It's time to change your response to his pessimism. Your goal should be to remain optimistic while not buying into his efforts to get you to persuade him to think on the bright side.

PUT A BOUNDARY BETWEEN HIS GLOOM AND YOUR OPTIMISM

Expressing your sympathy for his habit of bathing himself in pessimism helps you create a boundary between his gloom and your optimism. Here you're not asking him to look on the bright side. You should make clear that your world is not as bleak as his and that you're sad for him. Most importantly, you want to let him know that your world and his are different. No matter what he says, you're staying in a positive world with possibilities and things to look forward to in the future. But you aren't going to waste your energy trying to get him to look on the bright side.

Your message is that you are sorry he feels the way he does but you don't share his pessimism. It's best not to actually tell him that you are an optimist—better that it's implied. If you tell him, he'll twist what you say into an excuse to play victim. He might, for example, accuse you of thinking you're better than he is.

The most important point is that you set a clear boundary between your optimism and his pessimism. This boundary is for both of you to observe. It's too easy to drift into his gloomy worldview, so by setting the boundary with him you're clarifying it for yourself, too, as if you are reminding yourself to focus on the bright side of life.

IT'S EASIER FOR him to see what is wrong than what is right. You can help him by refusing to pull him out of his negative mood. Let him sulk alone and feel uncomfortable every time. He may not even be aware that his negativity is destructive. As you modify his behavior by ignoring it, you are helping him grow into the partner you hoped he would be.

You are also putting him on notice that the next time he says something that is pessimistic, he won't get you to do all the work for him to look on the bright side. You show him that you have insight into what he does to himself.

PESSIMISM OR DEPRESSION?

Some pessimists are depressed. In fact, pessimism is a symptom of depression. Pessimism can also contribute to depression. So what are the symptoms of depression? According to the Diagnostic and Statistical Manual (DSM) series that mental health professionals rely on for diagnostic consistency, the symptoms of depression include:

1. Depressed mood most of the day, nearly every day
2. Decreased interest or pleasure in all or almost all activities most of the day, nearly every day
3. Significant weight loss or gain
4. Insomnia or hypersomnia nearly every day
5. Psychomotor agitation or retardation nearly every day
6. Fatigue or loss of energy, nearly every day
7. Feelings of worthlessness or excessive guilt nearly every day
8. Diminished ability to think or concentrate or indecisiveness, nearly every day.
9. Recurrent thoughts of death

According to DSM, if someone has five or more of the above symptoms during the same two-week period, a major depression is indicated. This person should seek treatment. If the depression is not as severe as a major depression, there is the possibility of what is referred to as a Dysthymic Disorder.

Here are the symptoms of a Dysthymic Disorder:

1. Depressed mood for most of the day on more days than not for at least two years.

2. The presence of two or more of the following:
   a. Poor appetite or overeating
   b. Insomnia or hypersomnia
   c. Low energy or fatigue
   d. Low self-esteem
   e. Poor concentration or difficulty making decisions
   f. Feelings of hopelessness

If your spoiled man has major depression, you should insist that he seek treatment from a mental health professional. If he is dysthymic, encourage him to see a therapist.

BEING AN OPTIMIST FOR YOURSELF

If he insists that the glass is half empty, drink from the glass as if it is full. Don't bother trying to convince him that it's more than half full. He'll dispute anything that you say that is positive. You want your message implied by your behavior. Here actions speak louder than words. You want to define your perspective not by saying so but by behaving so.

> IT IS NOT your job to make things right for *The Pessimist,* although he would like you to believe it is. Maybe someone else (like his mom) always provided the positive in his life up to this point, but that doesn't mean you have to take up where she left off. If he doesn't appreciate the bright side of life, don't point it out. And don't listen to him tell you about the dark side.

Sometimes with a pessimist you'll need to spend time by yourself. You want to allow yourself enough time and energy to stir up positive feelings by your own actions. By this I mean that the time you spend by yourself allows you to develop your own feelings about an activity, uncolored by his. To get started, it's best to engage in a soothing activity that brings you a sense of happiness or good humor.

SUMMING UP THE PESSIMIST

He plays the pessimist in order to get you to do all the work to make things better for him in the future, but things never get better. By complaining about possible negative outcomes to whatever you suggest, he encourages you to convince him that all will be well. The harder you try to convince him to be optimistic, the more stubbornly he'll be pessimistic. Since you don't want to give him justification to be pessimistic, you try to prove him wrong. You work hard to come up with plans that will go beyond his pessimistic expectations. Avoid this, because it is the best way to reinforce his negative behavior!

Your plan needs to exclude trying to be optimistic for him. Be optimistic for yourself. Let him get sick of his own pessimism. To make this happen, you must "move out of the way" and give him the opportunity to learn to develop optimism himself.

CHAPTER 6

checkup quiz
Remaining Optimistic with a Pessimist

1. If you are going to dinner and he says that he doesn't have high hopes for the restaurant, you should:
   a. Tell him that it will be okay.
   b. Say, "Well, then pick one that you do have high hopes for."
   c. Be silent and hope that it will please him.
   d. Keep coming up with suggestions in the hope that he does have "high hopes" for a different restaurant that you choose.

2. If he prides himself on being a pessimist:
   a. Respond by saying, "Well, that makes it easy for you, then."
   b. Wonder if he had some type of trauma that made him that way and therefore he now needs your support.
   c. Try to match his pessimism by being pessimistic yourself.
   d. Consider the wisdom of his pessimism.

3. As you struggle to come up with vacation ideas that he won't shoot down with a pessimistic comment such as "It will be too crowded" or "The weather is always bad":
   a. Think of him like a slot machine: sooner or later you'll hit the jackpot with a suggestion that he won't complain about.
   b. Tell him that it's his turn to come up with an "optimistic" plan.
   c. Check the weather reports and call a travel agent to find out where the weather is great and there are few people.
   d. Don't even bother to count on vacations.

4. When there are a few clouds in the sky and he says, "Oh no—it's going to rain," say:
   a. "The wind will blow those clouds away."
   b. "It looks like you're really bothered by those clouds."
   c. "Yeah. Looks like a hurricane is coming."
   d. "Don't worry, honey. There are only two clouds."

5. If he tells you that he's not sure if you'll be able to drive to the next town because you're low on gas, despite the fact that it's ten miles away and you have a quarter tank left, say:
   a. "We've got plenty."
   b. "If you want to fill it up before going, go ahead."
   c. "Yes, we'd better stay home."
   d. "Honey, it's not exactly like we have a Hummer."

6. When you ask him if he would like to go to the beach and he shrugs his shoulders and says, "It's probably foggy," say:
   a. "I'm sure it's sunny."
   b. "There's no way of knowing for sure."
   c. "It should be miserable out there."
   d. "If it is you can blame me."

7. When you look out at the spring flowers in your garden and he says, "They won't last with the hot weather coming," say:
   a. "You're right. We ought to dig them up right away."
   b. "They'll burn up in the heat. I don't know why we planted them."
   c. "Don't worry. I'll water them."
   d. "I'm sorry you can't enjoy them now."

8. If he says of your new neighbors, "I don't see a bright future here," say:
   a. "Don't be silly honey. They'll be fine."
   b. "You're right. There goes the neighborhood."
   c. "I'm having lunch with them next week. Do you want to join us?"
   d. "They're nice people. Give them a chance."

9. When he shows a sour face in response to a suggestion:
   a. Keep making suggestions until his face brightens.
   b. Say, "What do you think would work better?"
   c. Apologize for making a bad suggestion.
   d. Get quiet and feel hurt.

10. When he seems on a roll with one pessimistic comment after another:
    a. Do your best to balance out each of his pessimistic comments with an optimistic comment.
    b. Throw up your hands and scream.
    c. Assume that he's in a bad mood and it will soon pass.
    d. Pull back from conversation until he is able to snap out of his pessimistic spiral.

7

Walking above Eggshells

A spoiled man often sprinkles "eggshells" around himself so that everyone around him is forced to tread carefully. He is practiced at being overly sensitive, so you get the blame for being *in*sensitive if you dare to criticize him. The crunching sound of walking on eggshells can be deafening. It echoes in your ears for hours afterward and that echo carries with it all the guilt that your spoiled man can instill in you.

He uses his oversensitivity as a tool to make sure that you keep spoiling him, by shifting the scrutiny onto you. If he can get you second-guessing yourself, you'll be too off-balance to think about anything else but what you're doing wrong. He'll set the conditions so that it always seems as if you are the one doing or saying something that's incorrect. And he makes sure you know that what is wrong is any critical comment about him.

ED AND ANNA

Anna initially came to see me at the prompting of her husband, Ed. He complained that she was rude and insensitive, but as she described her life with Ed, a different picture emerged. Anna felt as if everything she said to Ed was weighed, sifted, and analyzed for any hint of rudeness. She didn't feel that way with other people. In fact, she felt at ease with most other people, including casual acquaintances.

After twenty years of marriage, she had grown to wonder if she was repressing anger toward Ed that was leaking out without her realizing it. But she could never put her finger on any ill intent in what she had said when he protested that she meant to insult him.

There were times that she said the exact same thing to a friend or a family member and they would respond by laughing because they thought it was funny or endearing. There was, for example, the time she told her friend Peggy that it had been a tough day and she needed to hear only comical things. Peggy laughed and said, "You're lucky to have a comedian for a friend!" Later that evening Anna said the same thing to Ed. His response was "Are you saying that I'm a downer?" Then he walked away in a huff. She wondered if she had used a bitter tone or rude body language that she hadn't used with Peggy.

Twice she went into the bathroom and watched herself in the mirror as she tried to replicate how she had said what Ed found so offensive. The first time she did this, nothing she did—no facial expression, tilt of the head, or body posture—seemed rude. The second time, she went through the same motions and found nothing again. Then she turned on the fan to muffle her voice and tried to repeat exactly what she had said in the way that she had said it. Again, nothing. Then she focused on the content of what she had said and, remembering that it had been intended as a joke, started to laugh.

She stepped out of the bathroom. He glared at her. "Are you laughing at me?"

Anna froze. She didn't have a quick answer to explain away what she had done. "What do you mean?"

"I heard you in there!"

She realized that the only way out of the corner was honesty. "I was trying to figure out what I said to you that was so rude."

"That's why you were laughing?"

"I laughed because it was funny."

"You think being rude to me is funny?"

"It was a joke."

"You think I'm a joke?" he said angrily, then stomped out of the room.

Ed gave her the silent treatment during dinner. He avoided eye contact with Anna and answered in monosyllables when asked questions.

"Do you want to talk about it?" Anna asked.

"Are you apologizing?"

"There's nothing to apologize for. It was a joke."

"Back to that BS again, huh?"

Anna sighed so loudly that Ed took that to mean she had no intention of apologizing. He shook his head and left the room.

Feeling overwhelmed by being TRAPped, she stood up ready to follow him into the den to apologize. Then a surge of anger made her sit back down.

Developing a Strategy

After meeting with me two times, she decided that it was time to break out of the bind that made whatever she said become a reason for him to pretend to feel hurt by her crushing his eggshells. This was a tricky task because she wanted to have a discussion with him on a higher level than his petty eggshells.

Her opportunity to practice this new disengagement strategy came at breakfast after the second session. He had his face buried in the newspaper, only lowering it to take a bite of toast or a sip of coffee. As he tried to take a sip from an empty cup, he cleared his throat while glancing at her.

She knew that was her cue to pour him another cup of coffee. Instead of going along with his subtle command, she chose to read the paper herself. He cleared his throat again.

"I'm sorry honey, are you catching a cold?" she asked.

"No," he said with an irritated voice. "Is there any coffee left?"

He actually sat in a better view of the coffeemaker. She glanced back at the coffeemaker then looked back at her paper. "I think so. I bought a pound just a few days ago."

"I meant any brewed coffee," he said with a sarcastic tone.

She turned around to look at the coffeemaker again and saw half a pot of coffee left. Then she turned to him, seeing that he was staring at the coffeemaker. "It looks like there's plenty left. Go ahead, you can have the rest."

He continued to stare at the coffeemaker then turned to her, waiting for her to respond.

With a nurturing expression, she said, "Honey, you didn't tell me that you were having problems with your eyesight. We should get you an appointment with an optometrist."

"My eyesight is fine," he mumbled.

She got up and stood behind him to get a good view of the coffeemaker. "Oh, I see. There's a little glare on the coffee pot."

"Are you trying to ridicule me?"

"For having a vision problem? Why would I do that?"

"It's not about that!" he said.

She made an effort to look astonished. "I'm confused. What's this about?"

He shook his head and tried to gather his thoughts. This was becoming confusing and frustrating for him. "All I wanted was a cup of coffee."

"Well, why didn't you say so?"

"Do I need to spell it out?"

"I apologize. I just can't read your mind. Help me compensate for that limitation. Please do spell it out."

He left the room in a huff.

Holding to the Strategy

Anna knew that she would have plenty of other opportunities to be clear with him while walking above his eggshells.

He gave her the silent treatment for the next few days. Despite her inclination to make it all better and apologize, she managed to act as if nothing happened. She didn't respond with cheerfulness as she had in the past, nor did she match his icy demeanor.

Finally, he had enough. "Are you just going to be like that?"

"Like what?" she asked with a neutral tone.

"You've changed," he said.

"Thanks, honey. I'm working on it."

Obviously, Anna's challenge with Ed didn't end there. There is no quick fix and it took a consistent effort from her to avoid playing into his oversensitivity. Your challenge will also require a sustained effort.

TAKE THESE STEPS

1. Refuse to walk around eggshells and pamper oversensitivity.
2. When he complains that you've stepped on his eggshells and that you're insensitive, act as if you don't understand and he needs to explain himself.
3. Make his oversensitivity his responsibility, not yours.
4. Invite him to participate in direct, mature communication.

Whatever type of spoiled man he is, when he sprinkles eggshells around himself there's no way you can avoid stepping on them. Your task is to stay focused on yourself and what you wish to communicate.

Refuse to Walk Around Eggshells

You can only lose by tiptoeing around his hypersensitivity. The energy you waste trying to avoid his eggshell topics, issues, or behaviors can keep you from doing anything positive for yourself. That's what he wants: for you to be off-balance and spend your energy trying to avoid his eggshells. While off-balance you'll be so controlled by his eggshell technique that you won't know what to do or say.

Ask Him to Explain Why He Feels Hurt

You will probably feel as if you're taking a big risk by ignoring his eggshells. You don't know when he's going to hold you responsible for making that crunching eggshell sound. And you don't know when that crunching sound will occur. His eggshell oversensitivity keeps you tense and on notice not to upset him. Under these conditions, the natural tendency is to do whatever you can to reduce that tension. So you tiptoe around and make life as easy as you can for him. The more effort you put into making life easier for him, the more tense you become.

> AN *EGGSHELL MAN* reacts to any comment or behavior as if you stepped on his feelings. His oversensitivity and insecurity, coupled with his idea that he is the center of the universe, make it hard to be around him without causing him pain.

To make things even more complicated, he not only has eggshells placed in unpredictable places, but he doesn't always react to you when you step on them in the same way. Often it depends on what mood he is in at the time.

You can step on his eggshells by:

- Saying anything that criticizes him
- Changing the subject of the conversation even though he was barely participating in it
- Mentioning yourself, especially if it is something positive
- Correcting anything he says even though he asked, "Isn't that right?"

- Not being sympathetic to his complaints
- Not trying to cheer him up when he is grumpy

This eggshell tactic is powerful because it's so pervasive and creates an atmosphere of tension. Thus, you have nothing to lose by refusing to tiptoe around him. You're already tense.

Make His Eggshells His Responsibility

You must show him consistently and clearly that his eggshell tactic doesn't work with you. The message is that his oversensitivity doesn't get you to pamper him. He's not going to like it if you don't play along. In fact, he'll probably react more angrily than before to get you back into spoiling him.

DON'T FORGET THAT you have every right to be safe and happy in your relationship. If he's unwilling to accept that you're not going to tiptoe around his eggshells in order to stop spoiling him, it may be time to end the relationship and find someone who will treat you with the respect that you deserve.

When you do crush his eggshells and he looks at you as if you committed a mortal sin, don't buy the bad rap. Don't even wonder if you did something wrong. A guilty look in your eyes as you wonder what happened tells him that his eggshells have worked. Even though he's acting wounded, he'll see that moment of hesitation in your eyes and know that he's got you where he wants you. All he has to do is give you a glare and you'll be put in your place.

Invite Him to Communicate Maturely

If he can get you to doubt yourself once again, you'll become even more vulnerable to his eggshells. This will keep you guessing and you'll always be trying to avoid stepping on eggshells. Since you aren't always sure where they lay, you'll step so wide around him that he'll enjoy an even wider protected area. Now you're in a worse situation than you were before if you don't invite him to discard his eggshells and communicate with you in a mature, adult fashion.

USING THE CODE AND TRAPPED FEELINGS

Since you may be afraid to bring up things about the relationship, it is less **O**pen and inconsistent with the CODE. There is no balance of **E**quality between you.

Since your focus is on trying to avoid his eggshells, the relationship loses **D**epth. The relationship is only as deep as his petty wounded feelings. And since his concerns control the relationship there's no room for **C**ompassion for you.

The feelings of being TRAPped will be overwhelming. Try to use the red flags of feeling TRAPped to jar you out of side-stepping his eggshells. Pay close attention to the feelings of being TRAPped. Ask yourself if you feel:

- Tense around him because you don't know where the next eggshell lies
- Resentful because he has held you accountable for "offenses" that are unreasonable
- Angry because he puts you on the defensive
- Powerless because you don't know what you can say or do that will keep you out of trouble

HOW DIFFERENT TYPES OF SPOILED MEN USE EGGSHELLS

Each type of spoiled man uses eggshells to keep you off-balance. He makes sure that the balance shifts toward him. The bottom line is that by keeping you off-balance you'll be so confused and worried about upsetting him that his exaggerated needs will dominate your relationship. Read on to see how each type of spoiled man uses his eggshells to his advantage.

Pete's Eggshells

Even silence or neutral conversation can be a minefield that gets you in trouble. It's as if he is standing back and setting a trap for you. This trap is most often used by Passive Pete. You may eventually say something to shake things up so that the conversation can become more substantive. He'll passively let you say something that he can construe as offensive and then play wounded. Perhaps after a period of silence you say, "So how are things at work?" He responds by saying, "Did you have to bring that up?" He doesn't plan to do this consciously, it's just a tactic that he has developed to overprotect himself and get you to spoil him.

Passive Pete also uses eggshells to keep you knocking yourself out to please him. But watch out! He'll maneuver you into saying or doing something that will allow him to act wounded. As you unwittingly offend him over and over, the territory covered by his eggshells grows larger and more treacherous to negotiate.

Pete's eggshells crack when:

- You say something critical about him.
- You don't give him sympathy if he's ill.
- You fail to pep him up when he's playing downbeat.
- You don't carry the conversation for him.

CRUSH THE SHELL of *Eggshell Man* and you feel like you have crushed him and inflicted a wound. He prevents you from approaching any controversial issues, like asking him to make a greater contribution around the house such as doing the dishes or vacuuming.

Sam's Eggshells

Slippery Sam lays out mysterious eggshells. You never know what he's up to. His eggshells keep you from:

- Asking him any questions
- Saying that you don't trust him
- Accusing him of not telling the truth

Let's say that Sam came home late on Thursday night. Sally asked why he hadn't called to let her know that he was going to be late.

"Because I was too busy to call," Sam said curtly.

"Too busy? It would've taken ten seconds," she said.

He cast her a sharp and condemning look. "Are you saying that you don't trust me?"

She paused before answering, knowing that her usual pattern was to quickly deny his accusations. She knew that this would only put her on the defensive when she had nothing to be defensive about. "Trust?" she finally said with an inquisitive tone. "Why are you bringing up trust?"

"You were implying that you don't trust me."

"Now I'm confused. It seems that's what came up for you. I was just asking for the courtesy of being told that you would be home late. Now you leave me wondering why trust comes up for you."

She left him with that pregnant question to reflect on.

Mike's Eggshells

Magnificent Mike may seem so powerful that he need not use eggshells. But he, too, uses them to keep you off-balance. His eggshells are big and bold. These eggshells keep you from:

- Saying anything that doubts his "specialness"
- Seemingly aligning yourself with one of his competitors

- Implying that you aren't grateful for all of his help even though it's doubtful that he has given you any

> DON'T ALLOW *Eggshell Man* to label you as his persecutor. To prove you're not the oppressive tyrant he suggests you are, you'll probably react by soothing his imagined injuries and trying to make things right with him. Don't fall for that scam. It's exactly what he wants.

Tom's Eggshells

As you might guess, Traditional Tom uses traditional eggshells. In other words, if you step on him, you step on the tradition that he represents. His eggshells keep you from:

- Acting independently
- Saying or doing anything that puts him in a less dominant position
- Asking anything of him that he could consider feminine, such as doing housework

Tom would never admit that he uses eggshells, but you know that there are some subjects that are off-limits. He also reacts angrily if you upset his routines. There are things you can do that will set him off the way a match sets off a string of firecrackers.

REAL-LIFE EXAMPLE

One Traditional Tom had a habit of telling his wife, Nancy, that she was "listening to those people from the Left Coast again" when she would try to break out of her submissive role as wife. By that he meant California, which he assumed, incorrectly, was entirely liberal. She would typically deny it, saying simply, "I am not!"

One Monday night he plopped himself down in front of the TV just before the game.

"Honey, could we talk about Little Tom?" Nancy asked. "His report card just came and it looks terrible."

"Later, dear. This is my time."

Nancy saw a red flag, but she bit her tongue. Then she asked, "Are you saying that Little Tom and I don't exist on your time?"

He threw the sports page on the floor. "Don't give me that Left Coast woman's lib!"

She froze like a deer in the headlights. His sustained glare swept her out of the room. She finally slumped into a chair at the kitchen table.

She picked up the report card and laid it on a tray with Tom's snack. A few moments later, she placed the tray in front of him.

"Thanks, honey," he said, then glanced down at the report card. "What the hell are you doing sneaking that thing in here?"

"Sneaking?" she asked. "Sorry you've had a tough day. I guess I shouldn't have brought you urgent news about your son."

He grabbed the report card and his eyes widened while reading. "Damn teachers! And I thought you were helping him with his homework?"

Nancy felt like the wind was knocked out of her. She realized that she had naively thought that he would join her to develop a plan to help Little Tom. Instead, he blamed her.

"Couldn't you have waited until after the game? What's the matter with you?"

She realized that once again she was being told to follow his rules. With a sad and disappointed face she said, "I'm sorry. I guess I thought your son was more important than Monday Night Football." Then she left the room.

Later, as she brushed her teeth getting ready for bed, he stepped into the bathroom and said, "It was hard enough that my Falcons were getting creamed, but you had to come in and pour salt on my wounds during my time."

She looked him over, realizing that he was still reacting to the crushed eggshells. It looked like time for a nurturing comment with an aftertaste. "I'm sorry that your team lost. I'm sure that Little Tom will be disappointed to hear that. Unfortunately, probably more disappointed than he was from getting bad grades."

He looked stunned by her bringing the pettiness of the game score up in the same sentence as Little Tom. The implication was that he probably learned it from his father. But she didn't need to say that directly.

WALK ABOVE THE EGGSHELLS

Whatever type of eggshells your spoiled man uses, if he can keep you focused on his needs and neglectful of your own, then he's got you where he wants you. The only way out of the trap is to walk above the eggshells. That certainly sounds glib and is easier said than done. But once you learn how to do it, each time it will become easier. More importantly, his manipulation will become less effective.

So how do you walk above eggshells? Don't react nervously when he expresses his outrage that you stepped on them. He banks on your reaction. If you don't react, then the effect of his eggshell strategy will backfire on him. Make sure that when he reacts angrily to your stepping on eggshells, you respond with:

- Neutral emotions
- Astonishment

Be prepared: he might amp up his anger to get you to react by raising his voice. If he does raise his voice, tell him firmly that you don't deserve to be talked to like that. If he continues, walk out of the room. If he continues to raise his voice and is verbally abusive, you are dealing with more than just a spoiled man; in this case, you should insist that he attend an anger management program. You should never put up with that kind of treatment!

He doesn't want to believe that he is fragile or flawed. Instead, he wants you to believe that you're out of line. This is the key time to be consistent so that he'll believe that his eggshells don't work with you.

Ultimately you want him to doubt himself. When you show him that eggshells don't work with you, he will have to wonder why he uses them. In other words, he is left with himself, without you to overprotect him. He is standing there alone, looking at the mirror and needing to reflect on himself.

By refusing to react to his outrage, you shift the focus back to him. In this way, you're walking above the eggshells and not making contact. For him, of course, you're crunching on eggshells. But if you remain consistent in your effort to resist reacting to his reaction, you pull him up to your level.

HOW DO YOU react to *Eggshell Man*? Don't tiptoe, don't coddle. Don't accept responsibility for upsetting him when it had nothing to do with you. Don't confuse his oversensitivity with legitimate hurt feelings.

SUMMING UP EGGSHELLS

Eggshells are tools that he uses to keep you from either criticizing him or questioning your response to his spoiled behavior. Since you never know when you're going to say or do something that will upset him, you try to walk softly and tiptoe around the eggshells for fear that you might step on more of them. This only pushes you further into watching what you say and do. Then, because you're so tentative, the eggshells get bigger and more numerous.

Your plan should be to behave as though his eggshells are his problem and not yours. When he responds with anger or hurt because you stepped on one of his eggshells, you should act like he isn't making any sense. Make him explain himself. Make his oversensitivity *his* responsibility to resolve, not yours. Invite him to participate in clear and mature communication. Above all, you need to make sure that his eggshells don't succeed in getting you to spoil him.

CHAPTER 7

checkup quiz
Walking above Eggshells

1. If he has eggshells surrounding him, you should:
   a. Make sure to step around them.
   b. Ask him for help identifying where the eggshells are located.
   c. Be as clear and direct as possible about your point despite his protests that you stepped on one of his eggshells.
   d. Keep your mouth shut and pray that you don't do anything that upsets him.

2. If he complains that you crushed some of his eggshells:
   a. Tell him that you're sorry right away.
   b. Convey your sympathy that he is hypersensitive.
   c. Get out a broom and sweep them up.
   d. Pretend that you had no idea that he's oversensitive.

3. If he complains that you're rude:
   a. Ask him what you can do to be nicer.
   b. Do some self-analysis to discover why you are so cruel.
   c. Act astonished that he thinks you are insensitive to his feelings.
   d. Try to be as sweet as possible to make up for it.

4. If he uses body language such as a sour face, glaring eyes, or a hurt expression to keep you from saying things that upset him:
   a. Keep your eyes fixed on him to make sure you're in safe territory.
   b. Ask him what's wrong.
   c. Wear a blindfold so you won't have to look at him.
   d. Say what you need to say and don't let his body language control you.

5. If you know there are a growing number of taboo subjects, some of which shouldn't be discussed:
   a. Wear a rubber band around your wrist to remind you to avoid bringing them up.
   b. Keep an updated list of taboo subjects to know what to stay away from.
   c. Tell him that you didn't mean to forget which are the sore subjects.
   d. Tell him that there seems to be a growing number of taboo subjects that he reacts to and that you need to discuss them.

6. If he acts outraged when you criticize his ideas or opinions:
   a. Differentiate his ideas and opinions from his value as a person.
   b. Praise him for always having the best ideas and opinions.
   c. Tell him that you didn't mean to be so critical of him.
   d. Make sure that you never criticize his opinions.

7. If he dishes out the criticism but can't receive it:
   a. Put up a one-way sign and abide by the traffic rules.
   b. Chalk it all up to him just being more sensitive.
   c. Use a sense of humor when receiving his criticism.
   d. Let your anger build up enough so that it will soon explode.

8. If he subtly punishes you for stepping on eggshells:
   a. Tiptoe more than ever through the eggshells.
   b. Make it up to him by being overly nice.
   c. Ask him directly what's wrong. When he tells you, act surprised and make him explain.
   d. Stomp on more eggshells just to spite him.

9. When he gives you stone silence after you've crushed an eggshell, but it's evident that he can't tell you what it is because you'll find it ridiculous:
   a. Pretend that nothing happened and go on chatting.
   b. Ask him if he's feeling angry.
   c. Match his silence with your own.
   d. Tell him that you didn't mean what you said.

10. When he barely participates in the conversation, then winces when you ask for his opinion:
    a. Pretend that he really was an active participant.
    b. Tell him that you really don't want to know his opinion.
    c. Let him know that you won't continue to make all the effort and accept all the criticism.
    d. Change the subject quickly so that he forgets that you put him on the spot.

8

Detaching Sympathy from the Hypochondriac

A spoiled man may turn his physical woes into a way to get special favors. Whether he actually suffers from a medical problem (a minor one such as infrequent migraine headaches or a serious one such as a chronic illness) or would only like you to *think* that he does, he can use this claim to get you to spoil him. In this chapter, you'll learn to remain appropriately sympathetic while avoiding the risk of spoiling him.

Everyone deserves sympathy and support when they are ill. But if his demand for sympathy goes beyond what is reasonable, you're being asked to fill a need that can't be filled. It's as if there's no bottom to his container; the more you pour in, the more he needs.

He can use illness or injury to excuse himself from making an effort to meet you halfway on anything that you do together. Not only are you stuck with carrying his load, but you also drain yourself emotionally.

He can be extremely versatile in using illness or injury to get you to spoil him, by utilizing a variety of techniques including:

- Complaining of pain and discomfort to get you to drop what you're doing to care for him
- Stating that he's unable to help you around the house because of pain or illness
- Exaggerating the injury or illness to garner sympathy and shift you away from your own concerns
- Complaining of being injured or ill when he's not in order to escape his usual responsibilities

"OH, *POOR ME*" has probably received most of his lifelong nurturing by exaggerating his complaints of physical discomfort. Because of this he has never learned self-nurturing skills and is a very needy man who hungers for you to baby him. Though you may have a bleeding heart, make sure you can tell his actual pain from fake pain.

In the following story about Heidi and Ben, notice how she initially rose to the occasion and provided him with support. Gradually, however, he used his injury to get her to spoil him. She had to learn how to get the relationship back into balance.

BEN AND HEIDI

During the fourth year of their marriage, Ben sustained a back injury at work. Since he had been working as a carpenter, returning to construction seemed out of the question. His doctor recommended that he get retrained in another occupation before returning to the work force. Ben let Heidi know that he was daunted by the prospect of going through a retraining program.

Heidi had taken a second job to make ends meet. When she heard him say that he had qualms about retraining, she went into the bathroom and cried. She tried to hide her eyes when she came out of the bathroom.

"What's the matter?" he asked.

"Just dust in my eyes," she said, then walked into the kitchen to make dinner. She didn't want him to feel guilty about her disappointment. He had enough to deal with.

After he was first injured, she had resigned herself to making their life together work. She wondered if she had enough energy to continue working her second job. She didn't have weekends anymore to rest up before going back to her regular job. It was bad enough coming home each night and cooking dinner, not to mention doing the dishes. But working the weekends on top of that was too much to endure.

With no light at the end of the tunnel, she found herself wearing down. She caught a bad cold and a few days later he caught it from her.

"Thanks," he said glumly. "It was bad enough dealing with all this pain, now I've caught your cold."

"Sorry," she said.

Over the next few days she watched how he milked the cold for all the attention he could get. For awhile she forgot about the back pain. He seemed to have forgotten it, too. He complained about his stuffy nose. She had a stuffy nose, too, and couldn't seem to shake it because each morning she woke at 4:30 to go to work to beat the one-hour drive through rush hour traffic.

She needed to get to bed early, but by the time she finished the housework each evening it was nearly 11:00. Meanwhile, he sat in his easy chair watching endless hours of television, complaining that his head was aching and his nose was stuffy.

At this point she came in for counseling. She told me how hard she tried to remain sympathetic to his back pain. But his response to catching her cold got her thinking. She said that his doctor had suggested that he get out and walk but he always seemed to have an excuse. His doctor, who was treating him for back pain, also made dietary suggestions, such as avoiding sugar and caffeine, especially on an empty stomach. The doctor said that these suggestions could help make him less anxious and thus overreact less to the pain, but he didn't follow those suggestions either.

One Saturday after she came home from her second job she said, "So, I see that you didn't eat the breakfast that I left for you."

"No. Getting up and sitting at the table was more than I could do this morning."

She glanced over at the coffeemaker that had not been cleaned. "It looks like you could get up and make coffee."

"What? Now you're micromanaging me!"

She took a deep breath. For a moment she felt overwhelmed with guilt. The poor guy, suffering from all that pain; she was so cruel as to pester him about such a minor thing. Then she thought about what we discussed in counseling and realized that she wasn't micromanaging him. She was simply pointing out to herself how she had wasted her energy taking care of him when he wasn't helping himself.

"You know, I think I will help you if you help yourself," she said matter-of-factly.

"What's that supposed to mean? You're not the one who was injured at work! You don't have to suffer from pain."

"I'm sorry you're in pain. But you know what your doctor said about taking care of yourself."

"What does he know? He's not me."

She realized that she was on a roll and his reaction was less important than getting what she wanted said. She wasn't going to allow herself to be manipulated by his complaints anymore.

"I told you how hard it is!" he groaned.

"Yes, the pain is hard to deal with," she said, making sure to precede what she wanted to say by a nurturing comment. "And so is working two jobs, then coming home and having to do all the housework."

"Are you saying that you have it worse than me?"

She knew this was a potential TRAP for her. "No, I'm not trying to compete with you," she said without any defensiveness or anger. "But I am learning to take care of myself. And so can you."

Like Ben, your spoiled man may exaggerate pain to get you to do things that he actually can do for himself. He can take this to an extreme like Ben, to retire from working and leave the burden to you, but luckily most spoiled men don't go quite that far.

Nevertheless, as with Heidi initially, dealing with most hypochondriac spoiled men is difficult because their neediness stirs up a lot of feelings inside of you. His efforts to get you to spoil him for these physical complaints are directed toward triggering a variety of emotions in you, including:

- Concern
- Sympathy
- Desire to nurture

Though these feelings are natural and healthy in a relationship, they can be manipulated. Take the following steps to make sure that these feelings aren't used against you.

TAKE THESE STEPS

1. Keep your sympathy appropriate to the reality of his illness or injury.
2. Grant no special favors that appear to be beyond the reality of his condition.
3. When he tries to bring the focus back to himself with

endless complaints, don't engage in a conversation with him about it.

4. Center your focus on the entirety of your relationship.

Keep Your Sympathy Appropriate

A spoiled man can feign an illness or injury to get your attention. Since you can't see pain and discomfort, the only way you know that he's in pain is by what he says or how he behaves. Complaints of severe headaches and/or back pain are great examples of ways of getting your attention. Because these are types of pain that cannot be measured (unlike a broken leg or shoulder surgery), this is an easy way for him to exaggerate the severity of the pain. He uses the difference between what he actually feels and what he wants you to think he is enduring to get you to spoil him.

Because he can exaggerate his pain, he can enjoy your soothing attention without having to feel the pain. He may even get his doctor to participate unknowingly in this ruse. The fact is, most primary-care physicians are inundated with patients and have only a few minutes to see each of them. If he tells his doctor that he's in pain, how is the rushed doctor to know that he's exaggerating that pain? Then when he tells you that his doctor is treating him for pain he's bringing home "expert verification" of the pain.

> IF YOU ARE the "Oh, you poor dear" type, then watch out for the *"Oh, poor me"* man. Don't forget that you need to take care of yourself, too. Try organizing your time together in activities that are healthy for both of you.

Grant No Special Favors

When he feigns illness or injury, you let things slide that you would have expected from him if he were healthy. Instead of helping you do the dishes or picking up after himself, he now has a ready-made excuse why he doesn't have to help share the load.

All this gets more complicated when he actually does have a visible medical complaint. Let's say that he has a bulging or slipped disc. This can be a source of great pain, and if he does not follow medical advice to exercise or engage in a chronic pain class, then the pain can get worse. If he keeps this advice from you and instead plants himself on the couch in front of the TV, he may ask for special favors that he could actually do for himself. The truth is that chronic pain classes teach people to expand their activities and independence, not to contract them.

THE "OH, *POOR ME*" men use their illness or ailment as a way of manipulating the workload in the relationship. They are the men who believe they are entitled to be king of their castle. A king never vacuums the house or cleans a bathroom! (Especially if he is ill or injured.) Get him busy with the checkbook to pay some bills, or doing other helpful tasks that don't involve too much movement.

Don't Let Him Shift Focus Entirely onto Him

He may be ill with a cold or the flu. Here the symptoms are visible. Perhaps he has a stuffy nose. You may deal with your own cold as a nuisance and not a reason to close down shop or get him to take care of you. He may ask for full attention when he is ill, even when you are ill, too.

Take care of yourself

If you take care of him when you're also ill, that's a way to abuse yourself. You teach him that you don't matter. Why denigrate your needs to take care of him when he refuses to return the favor? You should strive for balance by nurturing yourself between nurturing him when appropriate.

USING THE CODE AND FEELING TRAPPED

All of his hypochondriac behavior wears down the CODE of your relationship. Mutual **C**ompassion evaporates because of his endless need to pull your attention toward him. There's less **O**penness because you don't want to bring up anything to upset him, as he is already "burdened." The **D**epth of the relationship stays as shallow as his complaints of pain or discomfort. Finally, there's no **E**quality because his illness or injury is the center of attention. Pay attention to the feelings that are stirred up inside of you when you feel TRAPped. You may feel:

- Tense around him because you're never sure how much more pain he'll claim to be in or how severely ill he'll claim to be
- Angry because he doesn't care for you when you are ill
- Resentment because when you spend any time on yourself he complains that you're neglecting him
- Powerless because you think that your situation is not going to get better but worse

GAUGE THE NEED FOR SYMPATHY

So how do you know that he deserves support and nurturance for his complaints of discomfort or pain? Remember the old saying "God helps those who help themselves"? One very important way that he can show you that his request for support and nurturance is appropriate is to demonstrate that he tries to help himself. You can tell that his request for help is inappropriate if he:

- Goes against doctor's advice
- Behaves in a way that makes his condition worse

- Asks you to give him sympathy when you too suffer from the same illness
- Demands that you serve him when you know he can serve himself

Here are some examples of spoiled men who asked for support for inappropriate reasons.

REAL-LIFE SPOILED HYPOCHONDRIACS

One spoiled man asked his family to sympathize with him because he suffered from an upset stomach, diarrhea, and hemorrhoids. Despite the fact that he had been told repeatedly that drinking coffee on an empty stomach in the morning made his problems worse, he did it anyway. In fact, he went one step further by using eggshells to keep family members from reminding him to change his bad habits. He said, "I wish you people would stop trying to play doctor!" He wanted them to sympathize, but didn't want them to attempt to solve the problem for him.

Another spoiled man complained to his wife that he suffered from a bout with the flu. His wife reminded him that she had just recovered from apparently the same flu that had been going around.

She said that the flu was a nuisance to her because she had so much to get done, which she managed to do anyway. He responded by laughing off her comment about the flu being a nuisance and claimed that it must have been a different flu. He then described in detail how incapacitated he had been.

She was far too subtle. She should have said something like, "It sounds like you're saying that the flu you had was a worse strain of flu than the one I had."

He might have responded by saying, "It must have been."

Her response would have been, "Oh really. Then I'm glad you didn't catch it from me."

If you offer sympathy and/or nurturance when you have or had the same illness and he doesn't reciprocate, pull back to take care of yourself. You actually do him no good to support his complaints while denigrating your equal status. Teaching him that you don't matter doesn't help him be a better person. It teaches him that you aim to spoil him at the expense of your own health.

> "OH, *POOR ME*" is skilled at getting the nurturing attention that he wants and doesn't deserve. If he can't get you to provide for him out of your sympathetic nature, he will go for it by wielding guilt.

In situations where you didn't suffer from the same illness and he asks for more sympathy and nurturance than you know is warranted, you should also pull back. If you don't pull back, he'll fail to learn how to focus on taking care of himself within reason.

LIFELONG PATIENT ROLE

He may be like many spoiled men who have used an illness or injury to give his life meaning. Unfortunately, the meaning that he develops turns out to be justification for him to play the patient. Even though you weren't the cause of his illness or injury, he can get you to feel guilty for not supporting his role as patient.

> IT WILL BE hard for you to resist comforting him if that is how you typically operate. Take a reading of the situation before you respond to fulfill his "needs." Pay attention to how you feel. The nurturing part of you will feel uncomfortable when another person is in need, but make sure that he really is in need.

I've met many of these men "working" the mental health system to get the mental-health providers to diagnose them as having psychological problems related to an injury. Their primary-care physicians become frustrated that they have used their injury as a means to milk the system and get out of work. Worse yet, they turn the patient role into an occupation or a source of identity, and no longer function as a worker and husband, pulling the marriage into a tailspin.

My job is to help keep a would-be patient from making a career out of it. This helps him regain his sense of self-respect. I help him learn to treat his wife with reciprocity and sensitivity. Despite the fact that some men remain injured and perhaps in pain, pulling out of the patient role and participating in a healthy relationship is in their best interest. You can help them see this by not encouraging their spoiled behavior.

SUMMING UP THE HYPOCHONDRIAC

The hypochondriac can use any physical complaint from a mosquito bite to a slipped disc to get you to spoil him. He not only wants your sympathy but wants you to do things for him that he can actually do for himself. If you are ill as well, he'll make sure that you think that his illness is worse and he can engineer it so that his complaints of illness or pain will focus your attention on him.

Your plan should be to resist these attempts and give him sympathy for only what is appropriate. Do not allow the sympathy to give him special license to get you to do for him what he can do for himself. You should stop acting as the caretaker as he plays his patient role. It does him no good and it certainly doesn't help your relationship. It's not healthy for either of you.

CHAPTER 8

checkup quiz
Detaching Sympathy from the Hypochondriac

1. If he complains that he is suffering from pain more than you would for the same injury:
   a. Think that he is probably more seriously hurt than you assume.
   b. Call 911 to get him to the emergency room.
   c. Treat him with respect and care commensurate with the reality of his illness.
   d. Tell him to lie down on the couch, then baby him.

2. If he shifts from one illness or injury to another and encourages you to sympathize:
   a. Comply with his wishes because he needs your support.
   b. Assume that he must be suffering from a chronic illness yet to be diagnosed.
   c. Think that he may be very sensitive to pain.
   d. Focus on the healthier parts of him and ignore the hypochondria.

3. If he goes to the doctor for a physical complaint then doesn't follow doctor's advice:
   a. Figure that he'll get around to it when he's up to it.
   b. Tell the doctor to lower his expectations.
   c. Support the doctor's advice and don't give sympathy to him for his resistance.
   d. Tell him that he ought to go to a doctor who can give him better advice.

4. When he becomes ill and brings up his illness in conversation excessively:
   a. Let him talk because he needs to get it out.
   b. Try to console him.
   c. Assume that the illness needs round-the-clock attention.
   d. Move to subjects that are more constructive.

5. If he goes to the doctor and you know that the doctor didn't agree with him regarding the severity of the illness:
   a. Report the doctor to the Medical Board for malpractice.
   b. Tell him that you will support his effort to accept the doctor's opinion.
   c. Ignore his resistance to the opinion and coddle him just as he wants.
   d. Applaud him for not following the advice.

6. If he doesn't go to work because he claims to be too ill when you know that he isn't:
   a. Call his supervisor for him and say that he is too ill to make the call himself.
   b. Grant him no special favors or sympathy.
   c. Think that he has job stress and should quit.
   d. Tell him that he really knows how to take care of himself.

7. When both of you are tired and sore from yard work and he complains excessively:
    a. Assume that he worked harder than you.
    b. Take care of yourself and withdraw your sympathy for him.
    c. Sympathize with him for feeling sore.
    d. Argue with him about who is sorer.

8. If he complains of being tired just before he's to do a task like the dishes:
    a. Do them yourself so that he can rest up.
    b. Ask him to do it anyway and add that you're tired too but you made the dinner anyway.
    c. Tell him that he's not tired.
    d. Tell him that he's been working too hard.

9. If he moans and sighs throughout most days without apparent cause:
    a. Tell him to lie down and take it easy.
    b. Suggest that he go to the doctor to get checked out.
    c. Tell him that he's getting old and should go out to pasture.
    d. Treat him with tenderness because that will help him stop moaning.

10. When he obsesses about a minor medical problem:
    a. Acknowledge that he's worried but don't support his worst fears.
    b. Tell him that everything is going to be okay.
    c. Tell him that he's a whiner.
    d. Consider that he might be intuitive and that it is a major medical problem.

9

Avoiding Destructive Arguments

If you don't get angry with your spoiled partner's behavior from time to time, then you're not awake. Anger is a healthy emotion and it's a natural emotional reaction to being manipulated. It becomes unhealthy when you fail to express your anger effectively.

A spoiled man can drag you into expressing your anger inappropriately. He can make the way you express your anger become the issue rather than why you're angry. At times you may feel so frustrated with his spoiled behavior that you just feel like screaming. If you do, he can say "You're losing it!" and ask " What's wrong with you?"

In this chapter, you'll learn to shift the communication rules to avoid destructive arguments and stooping to communicate on his level. You will learn instead to invite him to communicate on your level in a mature and levelheaded manner.

DOES *THE ARGUER* enjoy pushing your buttons and seeing you get upset? It's important to ask yourself this. Is it almost like he's toying with you—he's the cat and you are the mouse?

He can use your anger to his advantage if you're not careful in the way that you express it. If you are not clear, firm, and talking in a calm voice, he'll draw attention to how you express yourself rather than why you are angry. He can keep you from effectively bringing up his spoiled behavior by:

- Playing the victim of your "out-of-control anger"
- Shifting the attention to your "anger problem" and away from his spoiled behavior
- Putting you on notice that expressing your anger about his spoiled behavior is taboo
- Making you feel guilty about expressing your anger.

THE ARGUER'S BEHAVIOR will ignite your anger, there's no contesting that fact. How you respond will determine whether you have equal power or feel powerless around this spoiled man.

Another dysfunctional consequence of your anger, if you express it clumsily, is that he will engage in a destructive battle with you. Just like in an angry game of Ping-Pong, he swats the ball back to you. He'll complain that your swats mean that you're:

- Bitchy
- A nitpicker
- A micromanager
- Never satisfied

All of these gains for him add up to one big message: You lose if you express your anger about his spoiled behavior.

Notice in the story about Kim and Luke below that, despite her skill in communicating with other people, she had difficulty communicating with Luke without destructive arguments erupting. She learned how to pull out of those destructive spirals by not taking his bait.

KIM AND LUKE

Kim had been frustrated with Luke since after the honeymoon phase of their relationship because they weren't able to resolve arguments. She had grown up believing that things needed to be talked out in all relationships, at home and work. She saw her parents perfect this skill. They seemed to be able to talk through any difficulty, no matter how heated the argument. Kim was also a master negotiator at work—her peers even elected her their union president.

Unfortunately, when it came to negotiating differences with Luke, she fell short. She wasn't quite sure how to address this communication problem or even how to describe it. When she tried to talk through a misunderstanding or difference of opinion, an argument would break out, and she didn't know how to stop this from happening. These arguments often seemed to snowball—after a while she would forget what had triggered it in the first place.

She decided that an outside observer might be able to help her unravel the cause of and contributors to the arguments. She asked Luke to attend a couple's counselor.

He immediately responded by saying, "Why do that? The problem is that you're so argumentative. See the counselor yourself."

"Argumentative? I'm just trying to work things out with you."

"If we see a counselor you'll twist things around and make it all my fault. It's just like you do for the union against management."

"Are you saying that you're management and I'm the rank and file?"

"See, there you go again! Twisting things around."

Kim reflected for a moment. He had a point, she thought. But then again, she was also right. He did act like the management, though it was all very covert. He always seemed to get his way, and that usually happened after she gave up trying to negotiate with him.

Finding a Strategy

She decided that she would come in for counseling herself. In counseling we worked on ways that she could disconnect from being plugged into an angry exchange. She described how his sister, Sara, seemed to have mastered that skill with Luke. She was baffled how Sara was able to do it.

She told me that Sara and Luke didn't have the best relationship but since she was the oldest of his siblings she had earned his respect, especially after the untimely death of their parents. I suggested that Kim ask Sara out to lunch.

Bringing in Backup

As the two of them sat down for lunch one day soon after, Kim said, "Luke and I have been arguing a lot lately and . . ."

"You're not separating, are you? Well, if you are he's going to be leaning on us again."

"We're staying together if I can figure out how to make it work. But we can never seem to get through an argument."

"Does he play victim, punish you with those moods, and have a defensive comeback for everything you say?"

"You've seen all that too?" Kim asked.

"And any time you ask him to extend himself he digs in his heels and acts like he's being attacked?"

"Sounds like you know him well."

"He's my brother. Mom and Dad really spoiled him. Now he's gotten you to do it."

"But I'm already sick of it!"

"Don't fight fire with fire. I've learned to outsmart him. Just watch next time we're together."

Kim invited Sara to dinner on Saturday night. Luke didn't like the idea and expressed this before Sara arrived. "I don't see why you go inviting people to dinner without asking me first."

"What do you mean people? She's your sister!"

"Do I go asking people without checking it out with you first?"

Kim knew that this argument was going nowhere quick. So she decided to back off. "I guess we could call and cancel, say you're sick or something."

"No, the damage is done."

Kim decided not to respond to his strange choice of the word *damage*.

Dinner began with taut small talk. Then Sara said, "Thanks for having me over for dinner. This little diversion helps get my mind off my job stress."

"Bringing it up doesn't help you get your mind off it," Luke said with an air of authority.

Sara glanced at Kim and nodded as if to say, *Watch this. Here we go.*

"You're right about that, dear brother. It's time to bathe in your hospitality."

Luke shrugged his shoulders. Kim knew he was searching for a way to pick a fight but Sara left him no material to work with. By mentioning his hospitality she had also subtly challenged him to prove it.

As Sara passed him the salad, Luke said, "You biotech people don't know the meaning of job stress. If you had a job like mine . . ."

"Luke!" Kim interrupted.

Sara gently nudged Kim under the table. "You have job stress too, but you know not to talk about your stress," Sara told him.

Luke shrugged his shoulders again. This time he looked

befuddled. "You have no idea what I've been through," he finally said, as if he was trying to take control of the conversation and steer it into a direction leading to a bind for both Kim and Sara. He waited for one of them to argue with him or soothe his wounds. Neither happened.

"That's true, I haven't any idea," Sara said. "Pass the corn, please."

Luke took a spoonful of corn before passing it to her. "If only you knew," he said glumly.

"I don't know if being traumatized by hearing about it would be a good idea for me now," she said sadly.

Luke looked confused. He normally would have a comeback but Sara put him in another bind. Should he ask about why she would be traumatized? Or was she ridiculing him? Since she did not directly ridicule him, he couldn't accuse her of doing so.

"Wow, Sara. What's going on at work?" Kim asked.

"I don't want to bother you with it. It's probably a minor thing compared to Luke's problem," she said without a hint of sarcasm in her voice. In fact, she said it with a nurturing tone.

"Even so," Luke said. "Maybe we can help."

Just like Kim and her sister-in-law Sara, you too can learn to unplug from the tit-for-tat angry exchange with a spoiled man. I know it can seem hard to unplug during the heat of a moment, and you may at times need to neutralize the tension by bringing in another person, like Kim did with Sara. But the basic steps stay the same whatever the circumstances.

TAKE THESE STEPS

1. Recognize destructive arguing as a trap and pull out of it.
2. Resist his attempts to pull you back into arguing.
3. Offer the high road.
4. Argue constructively.

Make sure you express your anger and frustration wisely. Consider the following guidelines for implementing the above steps:

- Use a neutral tone when you point out his behavior.
- Stay away from "you" statements and make an "I" statement such as "It makes me feel . . ."
- Point out the *behavior* that upsets you instead of making a generalized statement about him.

THE ARGUER HAS probably triumphed by arguing through most of his life. He knows how to manipulate others into locking horns with him. He has developed the endurance and expertise that enable him to control and win most arguments. Change the rules. You have to learn how to avoid arguing by his rules.

Recognize Destructive Arguing

It's important to be attentive to how you slip into destructive arguments so that they won't undermine the foundation of your relationship. Destructive arguments drift off the point; they are more tangential rather than about the actual issues that need to be discussed.

The CODE gets thrown into chaos when one or both of you express your frustration inappropriately. Both of you lose a sense of **C**ompassion for one another. The **O**penness is marred by jagged barbs that you throw at each other. The **D**epth is blocked by the shock of the argument. Finally, there's no **E**quality because both of you have polarized into heavily defended positions.

You need to concentrate on playing by different rules. His rules are based on his efforts to hook you into a tug of war over who is the center of the relationship. If he invites you to play on the low road of destructive arguments, the CODE will evaporate.

In this case you'll be TRAPped, but can use those feelings to shift back to the CODE:

- Tension can alert you to be cautious when angry.
- Resentment can serve to jog your memory that it's time to learn from your previous mistakes.
- Anger can be the fuel to make your point as long as you do it effectively.
- Powerlessness can tell you that the rules of engagement must change.

Resist Being Pulled Back into Destructive Arguments

As your anger stirs when you are discussing your frustration with his spoiled behavior, there is always the temptation to throw in some emotional emphasis to what you say. Usually this will get his defenses up and spur an angry response. Pretty soon the two of you are no longer talking about the original issue. Stay focused on what you are frustrated with in the first place and confine your comments to that issue.

Even if you can avoid destructive arguments, you still may carry on the arguments in your head. If you still find yourself stewing about him, it's a clear sign that he continues to drain your emotional energy. It may be difficult to focus on yourself, and the time you waste imagining angry conversations with him can derail you from pursuing your own goals.

Offer the High Road

Remember the Golden Rule from the New Testament, "Do unto others as you wish them to do unto you." Your job is to behave toward him as you hope he will behave toward you. Untangle yourself from who wins by *shifting to a high road*. Your emotional energy should be directed toward inviting him to communicate on a higher level. Make it clear that those are your conditions for a relationship. If he chooses to ignore your invitation to communicate on a higher level, you will know that you did everything reasonable to make the relationship work and it may be time to move on.

Make a strong effort to communicate above your separate interests. This will be an invitation to him to participate with you in a balanced relationship. He may choose to reject the opportunity to communicate on the high road and turn your invitation into a negative. For example, he may tell you that you've changed. Yes, you have changed. But not in the way he implies. He regards the change as a move on your part to be selfish. In this case he is threatened by your move toward balance, away from him as the center of the relationship.

Your job will be to resist his effort to focus the relationship back on himself. A balanced relationship is what you offer. You must maintain the high road as your guideline to a healthy relationship.

Argue Constructively

Arguing itself is not a bad thing. It's how you argue that's important. You and he are going to have disagreements because the two of you are alive. That sounds pessimistic, but it isn't meant to be. The fact is the two of you are different people with different opinions. Those differences are bound to clash at times, but the true question is: How do you clash?

Ask yourself the following questions:

- When you have a difference of opinion, are you often put in the position of being the one who is wrong?
- Are harsh words spoken? In other words, do the arguments get insulting?
- After you end what had become a heated argument, do you remember what the original difference was?
- Do little differences seem to get complicated by tangentially related issues?

If you answered yes to any of the above questions, you are arguing destructively. You need to argue constructively. You need to make the differences between you fertile ground to grow together.

There are always going to be bumps on the road of life. As the AA bumper sticker says, "Sh** happens!" Constructive arguments can help you support each other during times of mutual stress by offering each other different points of view. They help you work out differences and grow together.

BALANCING THE RELATIONSHIP

Balance in a relationship can go from side-to-side like a seesaw but you need a central balancing point. One week or one month, you may be in need of support and a helpful sounding board. The next month he may need you to reciprocate.

What if you need support at the same time? He may feel that it's hard to provide emotional support when he's stressed, too. Yet, ideally, he benefits from a break from his own woes, which can only happen if he can focus outside of himself. He may also give some advice that may be applied to his own situation.

REMEMBER THAT *the Arguer* quarrels to get you to put his needs first by throwing you off-balance in an argument. Ironically, he wins whether you engage in argument or you avoid argument. You can survive this by arguing with him and by staying calm and focused on what you know is true.

GROW TOGETHER THROUGH ARGUMENT

You may laugh at the idea of considering an argument an opportunity to grow together. Before we get into some practical suggestions on how to make that happen, let's face some basic facts:

- You don't grow or change unless faced with obstacles or challenges.
- When both of you are open to each other's opinions, you allow yourselves the opportunity to expand, modify, or even change your opinion.
- By truly listening to each other, both of you will be understood.

IS HE THE type of spoiled man who always thinks he's right? No one is always right. Whether he agrees with it or not, you are entitled to your own opinion; give yourself that much!

Once you have made major changes in the way you deal with eggshells, emotional storms, and pessimism, it's time to cultivate constructive arguing. It's as if you are a gardener who needs to condition the ground before you plant seeds—turning over fresh earth and adding nutrients.

You may say that's all fine and good—nice metaphors and platitudes—but when you get down to real arguments, ideals such as these slip away. That's why you need ground rules.

Ground Rules for Arguing

The ground rules should include the following:

- If things get heated, you can call a time-out until the dust settles and you can focus with clarity on the real issue.
- Use "I" messages instead of "you" messages.
- Use active listening skills.
- Stay on issue. Don't bring up other problems even when you think they are related.

- Agree to disagree.
- Move on to compromises.

If you feel the need to widen the argument to include other issues, including long-simmering resentments about his spoiling behavior, take a rain check! If you are tempted to bring up things from the past, restrain yourself.

Arguing constructively necessitates openness without being offensive or being overly defensive. For example, when you are being attacked, you need a way to defend yourself without drawing more attacks. If you take his bait and fight fire with fire, you agree to play by his destructive rules. He may win the battle because he may be more accomplished at playing by those rules.

Your job will to be to change the rules from his destructive ones to your constructive ones. The most effective way to do this is to introduce a high-level message that will leave him thinking. You also want to draw attention to his behavior without stooping to the same level yourself. This will at the very least put him on notice that you pay attention. He may play victim and accuse you of the insult. That's where your neutral tone comes into play.

HANDLING HIS NEGATIVE JABS

His subtle and not-so-subtle digs at your character, such as "Don't be so bitchy" or "You're a nag," can accumulate. Sometimes they are hard to pinpoint, but they do chip away at you. A dig can be so subtle that he can easily deny it, or he can justify his comments by saying, "Well, you do nag about details that don't matter." Or a subtle insult can be so buried in the context of the conversation that to point it out may be turned against you. He might say, "What's the matter with you? I didn't mean that. How could you accuse me of such a thing?"

With each comment he has accomplished a double insult. Not only does he get away with the initial insult, but now he has taken advantage of the opportunity to insult you again. How could you be so mean as to accuse him of being mean?

Since it's a waste of energy to fight force with force, use a little impersonal judo. Let the force of his comment speak for itself. For example, say in the course of a conversation that includes a friend of yours she says something positive about you, such as that you often have a grasp of the "big picture." He might say sarcastically, "Well, at least that's one thing I can't accuse you of." What he is really saying is that you miss some details at times. You know that planning for your future together requires paying attention to the big picture, which he lets you do.

Don't take his bait. Respond with a positive comment and add a piggyback message to it. You could say, "Oh, thanks. That sounds sort of like a compliment."

He may respond by saying, "What are you talking about?"

You may choose at that point to call attention to his tone, in which case he will deny that he said or meant anything negative. Make sure to respond as neutrally as possible with something like, "Oh, maybe I heard that wrong. What did you mean?" At the very least this will alert him that you will not put up with subtle digs and that you will pay attention.

> YOU MAY FEEL that you are the peacemaker in the relationship and avoid conflict at all costs. Allow him the opportunity to be the peacemaker by holding your ground when you know you are right.

Try a paradoxical comment. Here you ask for clarification while simultaneously giving him an out. You could say, "I know that you didn't mean that there were other things you'd accuse me of." Here you are noting that he, in fact, did mean that, but you're saying that a courteous person wouldn't have.

Overall, when you focus on the CODE you go beyond the micromanaged detail of who said what when. You allow yourself to be free of the burden of micromanaging your own minuscule gains and losses.

SUMMING UP AVOIDING DESTRUCTIVE ARGUMENTS

Arguing with him about his spoiled behavior can seem like an angry Ping-Pong game. Every time you complain about it, he banters back. Eventually, you get so angry that he complains about the way you express your anger. Now it's your anger that is the issue, not his spoiled behavior. Participating in destructive arguments only results in you being thrown off-balance and more vulnerable to spoil him. After he points out that you lost your cool, you try to suppress your anger. While you're trying to regain your cool, he gets away with what you were angry about in the first place—more spoiled behavior.

Your plan should involve pulling out of the sidetrack battles. If he insists on arguing at this level, don't join him. He'll try to draw you back in; resist his invitation and communicate only through constructive arguments on the high road.

CHAPTER 9

checkup quiz
Avoiding Destructive Arguments

1. If you have a tendency to argue about how you are not meeting his expectations:
   a. Keep arguing in the same way because sooner or later he'll see the light.
   b. Change the rules of the argument and communicate on a higher level.
   c. Throw everything back that he tosses to you, like in a Ping-Pong match.
   d. Raise your voice to get through to him.

2. When he blames you for being rude even though he was the one who was rude:
   a. Apologize and consider that he's more sensitive.
   b. Believe that you were rude and get help for *your* problem.
   c. Work on communicating clearly and expect him to do so, too.
   d. Try hard to sweet-talk him into believing that you weren't rude.

3. When he argues with you every time you resist spoiling him:
   a. Remain consistent, clear, and fair in your efforts to keep from spoiling him.
   b. Give in and spoil him because it's easier.
   c. Try to look for loopholes in his arguments.
   d. Think that he may have good reasons to need spoiling.

4. When you express your anger in a manner that is inappropriate because you are so frustrated with him:
   a. Tell him he got what he had coming to him.
   b. Acknowledge that you did and state that you want to work with him on finding another way to deal with your frustration with him.
   c. Keep going with it because you're on a roll—get it all out.
   d. If he overreacts to your anger, turn up the heat and go one step further.

5. When you feel an argument is getting out of hand:
   a. Tell him that he's way out of line.
   b. Take a time out and say that you'll revisit the issue when you're both cooled down.
   c. Let the argument run its natural course and get it all out.
   d. Bring up the things that he did to offend you in the past.

6. When you're trying to de-escalate a discussion before it becomes a heated argument:
   a. Make "you" statements.
   b. Make "I" statements.
   c. Tell him that he's too argumentative.
   d. Shout "I've had enough!"

7. If he complains that you nitpick in your complaints about him:
   a. Tell him that he deserves it.
   b. Outsmart him by using a nurturing statement instead.
   c. Raise your voice so that your complaints are no longer nitpicky.
   d. Hold back your criticism because the situation is hopeless.

8. If he tells you that you don't know how to have a discussion without turning it into an argument:
   a. Tell him that it's really him who turns the discussions into arguments.
   b. Flatly deny it.
   c. Sweet-talk him down when he becomes angry.
   d. Tell him that you'll accept responsibility for half of it and invite him to join you in constructive arguments.

9. When you're angry and you know that you have a right to be angry:
   a. Let him have it!
   b. Use your anger as fuel and motivation to express yourself clearly and strategically.
   c. Bite your tongue, since whatever you say will come out wrong.
   d. Tell him that he makes you angry.

10. If during an argument he storms out of the room:
    a. Apologize so that so that he'll come back.
    b. Do nothing so that he knows that his tactic doesn't work.
    c. Shout for him to come back into the room and face your anger like a man.
    d. Follow him into the other room to continue the argument.

PART THREE

taking a stand
against *spoiling*

10
Asking More from Passive Pete

Passive Pete gets you to spoil him in discreet ways without your knowing it. He may act as if he can't control himself, let alone control you. But in truth, he's probably the most powerful type of spoiled man because your radar screen doesn't track his stealthy moves and red flags are usually slow to appear, if not completely invisible.

Whether it's through his intentional inefficiency or a tendency to force you to make the decisions, he makes sure that the buck stops with you. You get the blame for whatever was done or decided while he shields himself from scrutiny by excuses such as, "Well, it was your idea. . . ."

He tries to get you to feel bad about the decisions that you were forced into making because of his indecision, but the ways he gets you to feel bad aren't always obvious. He does this through grumpiness, the silent treatment, or muttering under his breath. The reason he often refuses to make decisions is that he doesn't want to be held accountable. When you point out that he put you in a position to make the "wrong" decisions, he gets angry and plays the victim.

Psychologists have coined the term *passive-aggressive* to

describe people who get what they want by being passive. Many people become passive-aggressive because their parents spoiled them. Others learned how to be passive-aggressive from a dominant parent who showed the power of passivity. This dominant parent let his family members do things for him.

> PASSIVE PETE IS also known as *Energy-Drain Man* because that's how you feel around him. He gets you to do the work in the relationship because he doesn't want the responsibility. If he makes the wrong decision and things turn out badly, he's to blame. So he'll avoid it and push it all onto you, slowly wearing away your spirit.

SELF-TEST: DO YOU SPOIL A PASSIVE PETE?

If you allow yourself to be trapped by these ploys, you're in a no-win situation. Take this self-test:

- If he sits back and excuses himself from making a decision, do you make the decision for him?
- After he complains about your decision, do you feel guilty for making the wrong one?
- When he gives you the silent treatment, do you do the talking for both of you?
- When you ask him to do something and he replies by saying "You better do it"—do you?

If you answered even one of these questions with a yes, you're treating him like a child. But even with a child you want to encourage initiative, right? By doing everything for him, you have invited him to sit back and passively complain about the job that you've done.

Many Passive Petes don't show up as easily on your red-flag

detector as other spoiled men. You may even initially think of them as "agreeable" or easy to get along with. That's how Paula misread Jamaal in the story below.

JAMAAL AND PAULA

Paula thought she had found her soul mate when she married Jamaal. He was unlike all the men she had known before who were overly macho and tried to be dominant. Jamaal was soft-spoken and never seemed to push his opinion or demands on her.

Over the next two years, the traits that she thought were so positive seemed to have a dark side. At first she couldn't put her finger on what was troubling her, but then those negative traits became dark clouds hanging over their relationship.

One day while on the way to the grocery store, he said, "Do you really want me along? I'm tired and not a very good shopper."

"I need your help. It won't take that long, you'll be okay."

"Okay," he moaned.

She delegated him a task to retrieve specific items. She had the shopping basket almost entirely full when she found him standing in front of a display of canned vegetables shaking his head with a sour face.

"What's the problem?"

"Well, it's like, what, do they think we're stupid?"

"I don't get it. What are you talking about?"

"Okay, it says here that you can get two for the price of one for this brand. But if you compare the price it's about the same as for two cans of this brand over here."

She looked at him sympathetically. "They overstocked a more expensive brand. That's all."

"Why didn't they just say that?" he accused more than asked. "You pick the one you want." Then he walked away.

While in the checkout line he looked down at the canned beets she had chosen. "So, you're really going to get that brand, huh?" he asked with a disappointed tone.

"I asked you to get a can and you didn't. Now you're complaining that I chose the wrong one?"

Paula's Realization

He stared back at her as if he had no idea what she was complaining about. It suddenly dawned on her that his passivity was getting more obvious. She wondered if she was doing anything to encourage it. Even with a matter as small as a can of beets, she had to make the decision! And he still managed to imply that she picked the wrong one. And he did all of this without actually saying that's what he was doing.

She vowed that she would do what she could to resist the impulse to fill in for him when he became passive. She thought about telling him that she was done with that part of the relationship. Instead, she decided that it would be best to change the way she responded to his passivity without telling him that she was doing it.

Paula's Plan of Action

That's when she came in for counseling. We worked on heightening her insight into how she falls into his passive-aggressive traps and also how she could respond to those traps to keep from spoiling him. She learned how to resist making decisions for both of them and how to detect when his pessimistic mood was bringing her down.

She got the opportunity to make those changes that night when she arrived home. She put some water for tea and asked, "Do you want tea?"

He shrugged his shoulders.

Ten minutes later, when she sat down with her cup of tea, he said, "I thought you were going to make me a cup."

"I asked you and you shrugged your shoulders," she responded then glanced back at the newspaper. She felt as if she should get up and make a cup for him, but resisted the impulse; she remembered that we had talked about how such actions would support his passive-aggressiveness. It was time to break new ground.

"Oh, thanks," he said sarcastically, then got up and left the room.

Her next impulse was to follow him to tell him that she was sorry. Yet there was nothing to be sorry about. In fact, he didn't even get up and make himself tea, which demonstrated that the tea was not the issue.

That night, dinner began on an icy note. He sulked, looking like he was mortally wounded. It was hard not to laugh and she was glad to be aware of and in touch with the humor of how childish his behavior was.

"Oh, broccoli," he said as she passed him a plate.

"I didn't know you don't like broccoli."

"You didn't ask," he said in a monotone.

"Jamaal, we've had it once a week for the last few years."

"I know," he said, as if he had suffered a great hardship.

She knew it was time to let him know how ridiculous he sounded without actually telling him.

"I'm sorry that having broccoli has been so hard on you. How did you survive it?"

"Well, it was tough . . ." he began, and seemed to realize that if he said more he would seem silly.

"And here I was torturing you with broccoli and didn't even know it. Kind of like the tea, huh?"

He nodded yes. Then he seemed to change his mind as he shrugged his shoulders and grew silent.

She let his silence fill the growing space between them. She made no effort to pull him out of his sullen mood. After her last bite of food, she got up from the table and said, "Well, I made dinner. I guess you can clean up."

He looked astonished by her request. "Thanks a lot," he said. "You're welcome," she said without an edge to her voice.

She had the lights out in the bedroom before he came to bed.

The next morning he said, "What's going on? Why are you giving me such a hard time?"

"Hard time? Being clear with you is giving you a hard time?"

"Clear? I have no idea what you're talking about," he said, then left for work before she had a chance to explain.

She decided to go out to dinner with a friend that night and left a message on the voice mail announcing her intention. When she returned home, he had already retired to the bedroom. She watched the evening news to give him time to turn out the lights in the bedroom. We had talked about how it's okay not to talk about such issues if she wasn't ready, and she knew that because she was not in the mood to talk, an argument with him would make it difficult to sleep.

At breakfast she said, "Carol and I went to that new restaurant on Main Street. It was really good."

"Not good enough to go with me?" he said sarcastically.

She looked him over, knowing that she had a choice. She could react angrily to his pouting or switch to a higher level. "Oh, are you suggesting that we go?"

"If you want, I guess."

"That doesn't sound too affirmative."

"All right!" he said testily. "Yes."

"Okay," she responded careful not to take his bait. "That sounds good. Go ahead and call to make reservations." She then got up and left for work.

You probably noticed in this story how Jamaal continued to try to manipulate Paula back into her usual pattern of spoiling him. These manipulations actually continued for some time. She had to remain consistent with him over more time than she had anticipated, yet it did get easier for her as she told him why she was changing her behavior.

Follow the steps below to learn, as Paula did, how his passivity gets you to spoil him and how you've played into it. You'll learn how to change the way you respond to him so that he will take responsibility for himself.

> YOUR PASSIVE PETE may have learned that he didn't need to make an effort to get what he wanted when he was younger. As an adult, he sought out a person who would spoil him just like his parents did. He chose you to fill that role. Now it's time for you to step out of that role.

TAKE THESE STEPS

1. Resist doing for him what he can do for himself.
2. After you resist, recognize the tactics he tries to use: implying guilt, instilling sympathy, or stirring up your impatience.
3. Restructure the situation so that he gains only if he acts.
4. When he finally does act yet continues to blame you for not doing it for him, reject the blame and praise him for acting.

> ENERGY-DRAIN MAN EXPECTS you to initiate his mood changes for him. That's a tall order for you day after day. If that's not bad enough, he may also resent you for trying to make him feel positive about whatever he is viewing as negative. What a double energy drain for you!

Applying the Steps

Notice how in the next story Gwen follows the steps outlined above: she pulls out of the decision-making role with Chris. Though he tries hard to get her back into that role by attempting to instill sympathy, she succeeds in making his reluctance to make decisions cost him what he wants. So he learns that he has to act in order to gain.

GWEN AND CHRIS

After ten years of marriage, Gwen decided that she had to get to the bottom of why she felt so frustrated with Chris. She had expressed her anger at him during the previous few years, but she couldn't put her finger on why she was angry. Chris responded to her vague complaints by implying that she had an anger problem and that she was victimizing him yet again.

One of her sources of anger was that she had been the one to plan all the family vacations and he had complained about each one. When she tried to enlist his help to plan the next one, he responded by saying, "You know I'm busy with work."

"I work, too," she responded.

"Yeah, but you don't have a big report to do and your boss isn't a jerk like mine."

Gwen had met Chris's boss several times and never could understand why Chris complained about him. Also, her job as a middle-school teacher was just as demanding as his. She had several deadlines coming up.

After coming in for counseling, she decided that she wasn't going to accept his excuses anymore. I helped her solve the problem while avoiding confronting him directly about it. She understood that if she confronted him directly, he'd play the victim.

Resist Doing Things for Him

At dinner one night, Gwen said, "I sure can sympathize with the stress of putting out that report. My classroom is one of the ones chosen for a review by the superintendent. It looks like the two of us are both too busy to plan for a vacation."

"Oh," he responded with a disappointed tone. "Maybe after your review?"

"No, it'll be too late. It's in May. When is your report due?"

"Ah . . . it's ah . . . due in April. But . . . then there's the follow-up."

"Follow-up?" she asked in as neutral a voice as possible.

"Yeah, the ah . . . questions . . . things that come up. And besides there's the recuperation."

"Recuperation?"

"You know, it's a big job, and I'll be spent."

Recognize His Attempt to Change Your Mind

"Oh," she said looking perplexed, but making sure that she didn't appear angry. She wanted to imply that she was bewildered. She knew that if she stepped on one of his many eggshells, the ridiculousness of what he was saying would be blocked out by his feelings of victimization.

"Well, maybe next year there will be time to plan a vacation," she said.

"But we can still plan something, can't we?" he said, now with an edge of desperation in his voice.

"Maybe. But it looks like you won't have time to plan anything."

"I'll help you."

She knew that every time he said he'd help, he always found excuses for his marginal efforts.

"Thanks, but I'd rather be the one to help *you*. Just let me know if you have time," she said, then left the room.

For the next several days, he sulked around the house after work. But Gwen didn't take the bait. She resisted the impulse to ask him what was wrong. She knew quite well that in the past the only thing that lifted his mood was for her to make it up to him. And then she would be obligated to plan the vacation.

When he said that he didn't want to go to the movies as

they usually did on Friday nights, she decided to go by herself. At first she felt awkward, but soon found herself enjoying the movie. In fact, she was relieved that she didn't have to hear him complain about her choice of the movie.

When she returned home, he was even sulkier. So she grabbed the novel she had been reading and went to the den. He soon came into the den and gave her the silent treatment. So she called her friend Patricia and told her how much she had enjoyed the movie, then went to bed.

Gwen held her own for the next week, despite the icy atmosphere. Then Chris asked, "So you're going to be like that?"

"Like what?" she answered with a neutral tone.

"Going on like nothing happened."

She knew he was asking her to spell out her mistakes and to apologize. She responded by asking, "What happened?"

He shook his head in frustration as if she had let him down.

"It looks like you're not feeling up to going to the movies again tonight," she said.

"What do you think?" he answered sarcastically.

She nodded, again neutrally. "Maybe Patricia wants to go instead."

"You'd do that?" he said, acting hurt.

"Do what?" she answered and walked to the phone. "Well, if you're not up to it . . ."

"I am," he said with a scowl.

Restructure the Situation: He Gains if He Acts

"Oh, that's good," she responded. "You pick the movie while I go take a shower and get ready."

"I don't . . ." he began. But Gwen was already in the bathroom before he finished his sentence.

Like Chris, your spoiled man may manipulate you on seemingly innocuous levels such as choosing a place to go out to dinner. Perhaps he says, "Oh, I don't know the area, you're better at choosing restaurants." If you choose the restaurant and the food is disappointing, he's not to blame. Since you chose the restaurant you may feel compelled to apologize. But you only made the suggestion because he refused to stick his neck out!

Try turning the tables on him. Since he said, "You choose better than I," you can say, "Oh, that's generous of you to say that, especially since the last restaurant I chose didn't work out so well. And come to think of it, neither did the one before it."

"What do you mean?" he says. "They were okay . . . I guess."

"No," you say. "Don't you remember how you didn't like the waiter at the Thai restaurant? And then at the Italian restaurant, you thought the pasta was mushy. Anyway, thanks for the encouragement, but I'll go with anything you decide."

By thanking him while pointing out that he criticized both of your last restaurant choices, you bypass his defensiveness and throw him off-balance. This technique allows you to leave him to reflect upon his behavior. It also gets you off the hook from making another "failed" decision.

Make sure that his passivity doesn't pay off for him. Since you've developed a habit of filling the vacuum left by his passivity, you've got to restrain yourself and let him take responsibility for himself. Without any defensiveness, turn his criticisms of your previous decisions into a reason for him to step up to the plate.

DON'T FORGET THAT he learned how to be passive. You can help him unlearn his passive ways by not rewarding him for being passive. As you fail to respond in the expected way he will begin to change.

REAL-LIFE EXAMPLES

Let's say it's a cloudy day; he may subtly put you in a position to feel responsible for the weather. He may give you a sad puppy-dog face or complain about the gloomy day while you're driving to an event that you've been looking forward to for a long time. You want things to go well and don't want him to fall further into moodiness. So you do what has become increasingly your habit, you encourage him to look on the bright side. Perhaps out of habit you say, "Don't worry; it's supposed to clear up in an hour or two."

The weather is not your responsibility! More to the point: neither are his moods or organizing his day so that he can passively let you make sure he's comfortable. He'll depend on you to do that all the time and won't learn how to do it himself. You may think you're nurturing him, but you're not. You're spoiling him.

Instead of trying to convince him that everything will be okay, go with his complaint by making a *nurturing comment.* Here you get to the heart of his complaint. This way he'll have to abandon it. You can say, "Oh, I'm sorry that the weather has got you so down."

He may respond by saying, "Hey, I'm not down. I, uh, was just making conversation."

Pause for a pregnant moment, then say, "Conversation?" in as neutral a tone as possible. Or you could use a perplexed tone to make the point that he had sounded as if the weather did bother him. You want to communicate that you don't want to listen to his whininess. But don't tell him any of this directly. You want it implied. He can't deny what you're implying, but he can argue with you and play the victim if you make the bold statement. This way you'll bypass his hypersensitivity.

Another Example

Suppose you go to the movies with him and the movie you had planned on seeing is sold out. You ask the attendant about other movies playing and find out there's a comedy beginning in ten minutes.

Meanwhile he falls into a grumpy silence. Your first impulse is to ask him what's wrong. Fortunately, you remember to restrain yourself. You ask him if he wants to see the comedy.

"I don't know, it's not the movie I wanted to see," he says in a somber tone.

"Well, I could use a good comedy right now. I'm sorry that you don't need one," you say.

"What makes you think I don't need one?"

"Oh, do you?" you ask with a reflective question.

"Well, after that disappointment, what do you think?"

Instead of answering the last little whiney jab, say, "Great, go pay for the tickets, the movie is about to start."

THIS SPOILED MAN was probably drawn to you for your positive outlook and your responsible nature. But what do you get in return? Just because he's not bossy doesn't mean he's not destructive to your relationship. With him balance is off, flexibility and empathy are in short supply. Don't do his work for him.

SUMMING UP PASSIVE PETE

Passive Pete gets you to spoil him not by what he does, but by what he *doesn't* do; he creates a vacuum for you to fill. He entices you to do for him what he secretly refuses to do for himself. What makes him so powerful is that he doesn't come right out and say "Please spoil me" as some other spoiled men seem to do.

Your plan should be to force him into being active instead of passive. You have a better chance of accomplishing this by boxing him into a situation that forces him to act, without telling him that that is your plan. Structure a situation that forces him to fill the vacuum of his passivity himself, without you filling in for him.

CHAPTER 10

checkup quiz
Asking More from Passive Pete

1. If he refuses to make the decisions affecting both of you, you should:
   a. Make them for both of you.
   b. Assume that he is not confident enough to make decisions, so have sympathy for him.
   c. Put him in a bind so that he must make decisions.
   d. Use the opportunity to make your decisions rule.

2. If he complains of a decision that you've made:
   a. Make better decisions.
   b. Try to convince him that the decision was a good one.
   c. Feel very guilty.
   d. Ask him what would have been a better decision.

3. If he gets quiet during a conversation and you know something that you've said bothers him:
   a. Change the subject.
   b. Say, "It looks like you don't feel like talking."
   c. Tell him a joke to get him in a better mood.
   d. Tell him you're sorry for being rude, even though you know that you haven't been rude.

4. If he contributes less than you and complains that you aren't contributing enough:
   a. Contribute more still, in the hope that he will notice.
   b. Put him in a bind so that to gain anything he must contribute more.
   c. Figure that your contribution is not as good as his.
   d. Quietly feel resentful.

5. When he complains about a situation that both of you must endure:
   a. Tell him that you are sorry that he is traumatized and thinks he is the only one who is bothered by the situation.
   b. Set aside your frustration in order to make him feel good.
   c. Assume that he is more sensitive than you.
   d. Listen to him so he can get it out of his system.

6. When he sits back passively when it's time for both of you to make an effort:
   a. Do his work for him because he must be tired.
   b. Specify your half of the tasks and tell him that you won't do his. Then complete yours.
   c. Tell him that you're fed up and don't do anything.
   d. Figure that he won't do a good job anyway and ask him if he would let you do his work for him.

7. When he completes something that you didn't have time for and brings it up continually as a way to get endless credit:
   a. Give him praise until he feels satiated.
   b. Acknowledge his contribution and let him know that it's that kind of effort that you expect consistently.
   c. Figure that he's paid his dues for a while and you require no more of him.
   d. Thank him for his effort and tell him that he's generous.

8. When he tells you that you talk too much and then when you get quiet he complains that you're not saying anything:
   a. Tell him that you'll be glad to participate in conversation that he contributes to equally.
   b. Do your best to find the right balance between being talkative and being quiet.
   c. Assume that you have poor social skills.
   d. Thank him for the generous feedback.

9. When he pays lip service to your concerns then quickly complains that something is not right for him:
   a. Be glad that he has made an effort to pay lip service.
   b. Let him know that words without deeds are cheap.
   c. Assume that he means well and that his concerns are greater.
   d. Offer him lip service back.

10. When you get frustrated with his passivity:
    a. Assume that he is all to blame and you don't encourage it.
    b. Acknowledge that you are a participant by discouraging his passive behavior.
    c. Believe that's just the way he "is" and won't change.
    d. Pick up the slack.

11

Holding Slippery Sam Accountable

You remember Slippery Sam: smooth and charming, he plays fast and loose with the facts. He overspends on himself, and you find out about it only by accident. He distorts the truth about himself, but insists on knowing the truth from you.

I've heard women complain that Slippery Sams have lied about very serious things, such as whether or not they stopped at the casino or paid the mortgage. Others tell me about Sams who lie about innocuous things, such as the store being out of milk when they actually forgot to pick it up.

One woman told me that her boyfriend always conveniently forgot his wallet when they met for lunch. Not only did he put her in a position to pay for his lunch but he also pretended to forget to pay her back.

A Slippery Sam challenges you to stay on your toes. He asks you to trust him as you brace yourself for the next discovery. Nothing is as it seems, but if you point that out to him, he implies that it's in your head.

> SLIPPERY SAM, AKA *Entitled Man,* feels entitled to be taken care of and entitled to treat himself to the things he believes he deserves. He's sharp enough to realize that he may be the only man you know who gets away with this, so he hides the truth from you while rewarding himself.

A Slippery Sam tends to lack a sense of responsibility. He wants you to be the responsible one. He may let you be the principal breadwinner or the one who has to make sure that ends meet. Either way, you are the one left to worry all the time over whether the bills are being paid. If he can get you to believe that he is doing everything he can do to contribute, you won't ask him to share the responsibility. Consider the story of Aliya and Rob.

ALIYA AND ROB

A year after her divorce to a man much older than she, Aliya started seeing Rob, a man much younger. Initially, the shift to a younger man revitalized her. Rob seemed on the go all the time and she liked the excitement.

She had a sizable settlement from her divorce, which she used to fund frequent weekend getaways with Rob. He never offered to reciprocate, and even when they went out for lunch, he let her pay. She knew he was "between jobs," so she didn't give it a second thought.

Within a month, he asked her to marry him. She paid for their honeymoon in Paris. The first year of their marriage seemed to go okay, but then when Rob extended his "between jobs" status, it began to wear thin. So she asked him about his effort to get a job.

He responded by saying, "The only jobs that are open don't pay very well."

She looked at him, dumbfounded. After taking a few deep breaths to quell her anger she said, "Do they pay better than the one you have now?"

He stood up from his easy chair. "Don't you get it? If I take one of them, I won't be available to take one that I'm more suited for."

She stared at him, trying to decide if that made any sense or if he was making excuses. She thought that she would give him the benefit of the doubt. Her mother always taught her to see the best in a person. So she did what came natural to her: she believed him. Why doubt him so early in the relationship?

The months flipped by. She was so absorbed in her projects at work that she didn't notice that Rob went sailing every day. When she asked him how the job search was going he said, "I think I'm getting closer to something with the company I told you about."

Aliya tried to remember which company he meant because there had been many. The next morning Rob left for a day of sailing. He had invited her to go along, but she had to go into work on her day off to complete a project.

Aliya's Red Flags

When she arrived home, she prepared a romantic dinner. Since he said he would be home at six, she set the table and had dinner ready. A half-hour later there was no Rob and the food was getting cold. At seven she took a few bites. Then she put the two plates in the refrigerator so that she could pop them into the microwave when he returned.

He arrived home three hours later. "We had a problem with the sails," he said with his eyes failing to meet hers. "And then we had to motor back in. Sorry I'm late."

She shrugged her shoulders. "I've got dinner in the fridge. I'll heat it up."

"No, thanks. Scott gave me a sandwich as we docked up."

She smelled alcohol on his breath. "Did he give you beer, too?"

Rob gave her a sharp glance. "What? Are you accusing me of being an alcoholic?"

She felt off-balance for a moment. Then she realized that he had bumped her off-balance not because she was accusing him of being an alcoholic, but because she was the one asking him questions.

"So what's going on with your job search?"

Rob cleared his throat. "Oh, uh, Scott says that he can line me up with a job working on boats."

At least he was getting a job, she thought. She had been feeling increasingly pressured to make more money. Their checking account was running on empty and she wasn't sure why.

After a month, Aliya became even more frustrated because Rob always came home late. When she asked him why, he would have a different excuse each time. Once it was the rudder of the boat. Another time he insisted that they had tested the anchor in very deep water and couldn't raise it up again. The next time he said he was so involved in scraping the hull of the boat that time itself got away from him.

The Confrontation

This excuse got her thinking. She knew it was time for a polite question. "I didn't know you were certified to scuba dive?"

"What?" he asked. "That was off the wall!"

"You said you were scraping the hull and tomorrow you have to sail to the Farallon Islands."

"Uh, right . . . we put the boat back in the water after I finished."

"Oh," she said, knowing that he offered her an opportunity for a paradoxical compliment. "Wow, you work quickly."

"What do you mean?"

"Did you put the boat back in the water before painting on the varnish sealer?"

"Uh, no, yes, I . . . I, uh, did the scraping the night before."

Aliya took a long perplexed look at him. "Oh boy, I'm confused. Weren't you guys out on the boat yesterday?"

Rob looked like a deer staring at the headlights of a rapidly approaching car. Aliya smiled.

"What are you accusing me of?" he asked in an irate tone.

"Now you're getting me even more confused. Is there something I should be accusing you of?"

"Of course not!" he said hotly.

"Good," she said with an ironic smile, then left the room.

The next night he was on time for dinner. She knew his punctuality was too good to last. She was right. On the fourth night he was two hours late. When he walked in he had a guilty look on his face. "Are you going to get weird on me again?"

She gave him a knowing and disappointed look. "Do I need to?"

"There you go again!"

"Why haven't I seen a paycheck?" she said in a neutral voice.

"Oh, that again! Can't a guy get his life together around here?"

"Sure, that's a great idea. Please do," she said and went into another room.

Like Aliya during the beginning of her relationship, you may worry that you are too cynical or that you aren't giving him a fair chance because you don't trust him. The way to clear the air and determine if he really is trying to contribute to your relationship is to look for a pattern of him not contributing. The pattern can show that he is making a consistent effort or it can show that he's making a minimal effort to contribute.

AT FIRST YOU might not heed the negative feelings you're getting in your relationship with this guy, because of his charisma and ability to seem caring when he needs to win you over. Pay attention to how you feel *before* he works on you with his magic sweet-talk.

Let's say he's unemployed and he doesn't apply for some jobs because he is trying to find the "right fit." Or maybe he's fired because of "politics" or he quits because he didn't want to "play their game." Then he remains unemployed without putting forth effort to find a new job.

If, on the other hand, he is a victim of the new economy and his company downsized, he may feel like a used paper cup that has been thrown away. Your sympathy and support would be helpful. Yet he still needs to adapt to the realities in the workplace. If he can't work in his old capacity, he can re-skill and find work in a new capacity. If he seems willing to try, you can be confident that he is making the correct effort.

TAKE THESE STEPS

1. Hold him accountable for his slippery behavior. Consistently.
2. Listen with a third ear when he tries to explain away spending too much or where he had been for those missing hours and confuses you by his spun-out story.
3. Don't be influenced by his sweet talk; focus on the issue at hand.
4. Point out the logical consequences linked to the convoluted stories that he weaves.

To avoid being tricked by him, you'll need to stay not just one step but several steps in front of him. This is because he's probably experienced at anticipating how you may try to hold him accountable. He's got a ready-made way to slip out of the trap that he expects you to spring on him. By anticipating what he has up his sleeve, you'll be able to pull the covers off his spoiled behavior and leave him baffled. You want him baffled because that puts him in a position where his slipperiness won't work.

Most Slippery Sams have jobs, yet many of them tend to overspend and leave their wives worrying about how to pay the bills. Consider the case of Tania and Nick; notice how Tania applied the steps outlined above in order to stop her Slippery Sam in his tracks.

TANIA AND NICK

Tania and Nick had been married for a short while when she began to notice unreliable behavior from him. Both of their jobs seemed to demand a great deal of attention and overtime. One evening around 7:00 she had yet to wrap things up at work. She called home but he wasn't there. Then she called his office and only got voice mail. When she finally arrived home at 9:00, the house was empty. She called and left a message on his work voice mail. He didn't return the call and got home at 10:30.

"So what's been going on?" she asked.

"You didn't get my message?" he responded.

"No," she said, picking through the refrigerator for leftovers.

"I better take a shower now so I can get to the office early tomorrow." He slipped off into the bathroom before she could respond.

When she drove into the driveway the next night after work she saw a boat on a trailer occupying her usual parking spot.

"Do you like it?" he asked, beaming, as she walked in the front door.

"But I thought we were saving up for a down payment on a house."

"Sure. That too. There's a lot of overtime pay, you know."

"But you didn't even ask me!" she said.

Rejecting a Slippery Present

He hung his head, looking hurt. "I thought it would be a cool surprise." He glanced up at her. He saw that she didn't seem to think it was a cool surprise. "Kind of like we gave ourselves our own wedding present."

"How much was it?"

"It was an incredible deal. I, uh . . . we couldn't pass it up," he said, then led her over to the couch and held her tenderly.

She came in for counseling later that week. She was determined to put the brakes on a potentially destructive relationship.

Bright and early the following morning, she searched out the checkbook. Up to that point he had been handling it, and now she discovered that that was a mistake. There was no record of the overtime that he was supposedly working.

He stumbled into the kitchen and saw her sitting with the checkbook in front of her on the table. "Where's the record of the boat and your overtime?" she asked.

"What is this?" he protested. "I just woke up and you're attacking me?"

"I don't feel good about this," she said, wondering if hitting him so hard and so early in the morning was wise.

"You will as soon as we get the boat out on the lake this Saturday. Just the two of us."

That did sound good. But so did buying a new house. And by the looks of things, that plan was drifting away in a boat she didn't want.

"How 'bout spending some time alone with me, away from everything here," he asked, punctuating his words with a kiss.

Don't Be Influenced by Sweet Talk

Those words sounded inviting. She too wanted to get away. All the overtime and house chores were wearing on her. She wanted to rekindle their relationship. Yet, she hadn't been working overtime to buy a boat.

"Aren't we still working together to buy a house?"

"Sure we are, but can't we enjoy ourselves and each other on the way?"

That sounded too cloudy to Tania. "Yes, but what's the priority?"

"Us!" he said with conviction and tears in his eyes.

The tears almost got her. She wanted to float away with him in his boat. Then it hit. It was *his* boat and *he* made a unilateral decision to buy it for himself. Then he tried to convince her that it had something to do with their relationship.

It also occurred to her that confronting him head-on about it resulted in far more than a tit-for-tat argument. He was such an expert at sweet-talking her—he had her thinking that he bought the boat for her and for the sake of the relationship.

"So your top priority is us and you're willing to make sacrifices for the relationship?"

He nodded hesitantly.

"Good. So a home for our relationship is a priority?"

"Of course. And so is the time we spend together."

She knew he was trying to position himself to equate the boat and the house. Her next step meant that she could use his own words to corner him. "That's good. Because where we live is where we spend most of our time together."

"Are you trying to say that I should take the boat back?"

"Does it fit with your top priority?"

He looked away, trying to gather his thoughts. "I think we can do both."

"Both? You mean fit with our priorities or fit with yours?"

"You're twisting my words!" he said, looking mortally wounded. He could see that ploys didn't work, so he hugged her. "Honey, the boat is for you. You've been working so hard doing all that overtime."

"So, I've been the only one really working overtime?"

He jumped to his feet and looked at her with furious eyes. "What! You don't trust me?"

"Are you saying that I shouldn't?" she asked, careful not to deny it.

He left the room in a huff.

She was furious that he had bought a boat without telling her and had left the question of who was doing the overtime work unanswered.

Before rushing off to work, she called the bank to get a reading on how much he spent for the boat. There was no record of the transaction. Next she checked the account balance and did some calculations as to how much she estimated for her overtime pay. There was no evidence of his overtime pay.

She arrived home at 9:00 that night and he at 9:30. She asked, "How did the overtime go tonight?"

He looked troubled by the question. "Work was tough today."

She noticed that he evaded responding specifically to her reference to overtime and broadened his response to include work in general. Technically, he didn't lie.

Uncovering the Truth

"There's no withdrawal from our account," she said flatly as she set the table.

A stiff silence hung between them. "What are you, some kind of a detective?"

That accusation stung. She didn't want to be in a position of having to check up on him, but she did want him to believe that she didn't trust him. She just didn't want to say it. So she let his accusation go unanswered.

"Maybe the withdrawal didn't get processed yet by the bank," he suggested.

After another long pause, he admitted, "I paid for it with our credit card."

"What card?" she asked, "I thought we agreed to just have one card."

"No," he said, looking surprised. "What about the Visa?"

"Where is it? I don't have a copy."

"You don't?" he said, continuing to look surprised. He pulled his credit card out from his wallet and handed it to her.

She inspected it. "What else are you not showing me?"

He squirmed into the chair at the kitchen table. "All right. I haven't been working overtime for awhile."

"And my overtime paid for your boat."

"It's our boat!" he said with an endearing smile. "And it's our other account."

She stood up, continuing to stare at him. "What are you going to do with your account and your boat?"

He looked back at her, apparently wondering if she really meant business. "It would've been so great for us to get away on the boat," he said glumly.

"It's nice to hear that you're ready to sell it back."

"But I didn't . . ." he began.

"And the credit card?" she cut in.

"I guess I'll give that up too," he said looking defeated.

After coming in for counseling, she learned to set limits with him. She demanded that he turn his credit cards over to her. To ensure that she didn't simply fall into a mother's role by doling out an allowance, she asked him to attend Debtors Anonymous. Then she moved on to graduated expectations that he manage the debt he had accumulated.

Overall, many women who have a Slippery Sam in their lives are like Tania. She had to consistently hold Nick accountable until he got it clear that she wasn't going to spoil him. He was very disappointed to sell back the boat and cancel the credit card account, but these were the first steps among many others that he had to take to begin to build up trust in their relationship.

DON'T ALLOW YOURSELF to get defensive or you will be powerless. Stay calm, don't let yourself get too heated. Take control by holding him accountable for what he says; let him know he is not fooling you with his jumbled tales or rationalizations.

You're going to need ways to cut through the lies to get to the truth. With a Slippery Sam, it's best to do this in such a way that he can't slip out from being cornered. You've learned that he'll look for any opportunity to turn the truth around on you and push you in the corner instead of him.

HOW HE BRAINWASHES YOU

Over time you may feel that what you thought was up is down and what was down is up. Many years ago, people commonly used the term *brainwashing*. Brainwashing described a process that manipulated someone to the extent that what he believed to be true was false and what he thought was false was actually true. Like the repetitive drips of a leaky faucet, brainwashing is accomplished by repetition and its effect is cumulative. Slippery Sam brainwashes you by continually distorting the truth and challenging your version of it. This can make you feel crazy.

What you need is brain clearing, not brainwashing. Your job is to make clear that you aren't fooled by his smokescreen.

Being on your toes makes more than your toes tired and can exhaust you emotionally. But you won't be emotionally exhausted if you can practice detachment. What I mean by detachment is that you should pull away emotionally from the little battles for the truth. By doing so, you'll show that his efforts to spin the truth don't make you feel confused. This doesn't mean that you don't challenge him about the truth. Rather, you detach yourself emotionally while you allow him to get tangled up in his story.

REAL-LIFE EXAMPLE

Suppose a Slippery Sam tries to blame you for putting a dent on the car fender that he actually put there. He may say, "Wow!

Did you see that dent?" Don't take the bait and say "I didn't put it there." You'll be setting him up for a slippery comeback. He'll say something like "Why are you so defensive?" He'll have shifted attention to you while you've seemingly invited scrutiny over your possible guilt.

Try a reflective question instead. Say something in a neutral tone like "Of course, you're not denying that you made it, are you?"

He'll probably respond either by saying, "Well . . . uh, maybe something happened." Or, "I don't know how it happened." Or, "If I did it was because. . . ."

Your response is key. Sound perplexed, not angry or defensive. Simply look at him with a blank or even stupefied face. If he still tries to slip out of taking responsibility for it, say, "When you're ready to talk about it, let me know."

Dealing with a Slippery Sam is sometimes like trying to hold onto a wet bar of soap. If you're too obvious when you try to hold him accountable, he'll slip away. Don't forget to:

- Avoid setting yourself up to take the blame for something he did.
- Ask open-ended questions and respond to his answers in an even or perplexed tone.
- Restrain your anger so that he doesn't use it against you.
- Leave him wondering whether you know the truth.

A MASTERFUL *Entitled Man* will bestow compassionate words upon you, but rarely will he give you the kind of gifts he buys for himself. Ever-selfish, he may even try to persuade you that something he bought for himself was truly for you or your benefit. Don't fall for that.

SUMMING UP SLIPPERY SAM

Slippery Sam gets you to spoil him by keeping you guessing. You're never quite sure what he's doing or what he's done. If he has spent too much money or been somewhere that he shouldn't have, he can spin a good story that explains it away. He thinks his ability to sweet-talk you and be charming makes it all better.

Your plan should be to cut through his smokescreen. Hold him accountable by making him suffer the consequences of the illogic of his spun story. Don't clean up after him. Make sure that it's him who does the cleaning up of his own messes.

A spoiled man can talk the talk. But you need to insist that he walk the walk.

CHAPTER 11

checkup quiz
Holding Slippery Sam Accountable

1. When he charms you after disappointing you:
   a. Figure that he balances out the bad with charm.
   b. Hold him responsible for his deeds.
   c. Try to decide which one of him is for real.
   d. Enjoy the charming part of him as most important.

2. If he tells you that he needs his "toys" and often overspends on them:
   a. Believe that a man needs his toys.
   b. Tell him to grow up, toys are for kids.
   c. If he can work extra hours and pay the bills, negotiate with him.
   d. Make it your responsibility to maintain his toys.

3. If he wants to know every detail of your whereabouts but is secretive about himself:
   a. Let him know what he wants to know and don't expect openness in return.
   b. Tell him to mind his own business.
   c. Tell him a little then ask him to reciprocate.
   d. Ask what he's hiding.

4. When he overspends:
    a. Shrug your shoulders and say, "Things could be worse."
    b. Tell him he's like a naughty child.
    c. Invite him to join you to balance the checkbook each week.
    d. Let him make up for it by his charm.

5. If he has a "problem" with not telling the truth:
    a. Assume that he's pointing out that there's no absolute truth.
    b. Structure it so that he suffers concrete consequences for his lies that stem directly from what he claims to be the truth.
    c. Track down every lie like a detective.
    d. Consider it a fun game that keeps you on your toes.

6. When he seems to have a glib excuse for everything:
    a. Admire the brilliance of his excuses.
    b. Argue the details of each excuse.
    c. Let him box himself into a corner dictated by the logic of his excuses.
    d. Ask him for some lessons on how to be glib.

7. If he complains that you don't trust him when you know that there is reason to not trust him:
    a. Tell him that you trust him implicitly.
    b. Tell him that you'd like to give him an opportunity to prove that he is trustworthy.
    c. Tell him that he's untrustworthy.
    d. Feel guilty and try to make it up to him.

8. If he has a knack of sweet-talking you into anything:
   a. Enjoy his sweet talk.
   b. Look beyond the sweet talk for the reasonableness of what he asks for.
   c. Tell him that you're deaf to sweet talk.
   d. Think of his sweet talk as affection.

9. When he tells you something that is untrue:
   a. Laugh and tell him that he's a good comedian.
   b. Don't believe anything he says anymore.
   c. Engineer it so that he contradicts himself.
   d. Argue with him about it.

10. When he puts you in a situation where you clean up his mess:
    a. Clean it up before someone notices.
    b. Tell him that he's good at making messes.
    c. Restructure the situation so that he must clean it up.
    d. Plead with him to stop it.

12

Humbling Magnificent Mike

Everyone has some positive traits. What you bring to your relationship is going to be different from what he brings, and all will be well if both of you appreciate and respect each other for these differences. Yet you're no longer an equal partner if his talents or status brings him special favors and if you get none in return.

When he gets you to spoil him for being "special," your needs get subordinated to his. It's this type of spoiled man that I call Magnificent Mike. He can be very persuasive at convincing you that he needs special handling and reminding you of his royal blood and your common origins.

> MAGNIFICENT MIKE IS *Center-of-the-Universe Man*. Although he would like you to believe that your life revolves around him, make sure that you share the universe as an equal partner.

Magnificent Mike thinks he's above scrutiny. He can't laugh at himself and sure doesn't want you to. He wants you to spoil him but doesn't want your constructive criticism. Consider how Barbara challenged Bryan to stop being a Magnificent Mike.

BRYAN AND BARBARA

Two months after their wedding Barbara and Bryan settled into the kind of relationship that she had not anticipated. They had initially been coworkers. Though they remained peers as computer programmers, Bryan would now often remind her that he was her mentor and that she wouldn't be in the position she was now if not for his help.

Every day after work he'd complain about the other programmers and how much he did for them. He said that they learned everything they knew from him. This was only partly true; he was the first hired and had helped train everyone, but since then, the others had held their own.

One night after work he said, "I think it's about time I get a little credit from everyone."

A Lopsided Relationship

She wondered if he meant that she, too, wasn't giving him enough credit. Over the next few weeks, she made sure that she praised him even more than she had before. After work she even gave him time to "unwind," as he called it. She didn't allow herself the same time to unwind because there was dinner to be made and dishes to wash.

Once she cleaned up after dinner, he often asked for a back rub, but never reciprocated. Physical intimacy in their relationship devolved into only him getting his "needs" met.

She assumed that he would eventually appreciate her extra effort, but after a few more months the situation only grew worse. She became so frustrated with the lopsided relationship that she came in for counseling. I told her that she would soon find herself in quicksand. "The more you give to him without getting anything back, the more he'll want," I said. "Then he won't think he needs to return anything."

"Don't you think he'll see how much I love him and love me back?"

"Love you back? Do you mean that he's not doing that now?"

A Plan of Action

Barbara was stunned by her own revelation. We talked about the various methods that she could use to get her relationship into balance. She agreed that it was time to talk to him, and that night, when he asked for his usual back rub, the opportunity presented itself. She leaned down to begin, then abruptly stood back up.

"What's the matter?" he said.

"I pulled a muscle in my shoulder," she said, wincing in pain, though she hadn't really pulled a muscle.

"If you move your arm back and forth it will loosen up and be fine."

She tried to move her arm around with a windmill motion, careful to grimace every inch of the way. "No, it's still there."

He sighed. It looked to her that he was more disappointed that he wasn't going to get an immediate back rub than he was concerned that she had hurt her shoulder.

"Could you rub my shoulder?" she asked.

"Sure," he said, with unconvincing enthusiasm.

She let him begin to rub her shoulder, relieved that it was easy to turn things around. But he stopped as quickly as he began. "Try that," he said.

She moved her arm around and made sure to grimace again.

"Well, I think it will get better in time," he said. "Why don't you give my back a try?"

At first Barbara thought he was kidding. He hadn't even given her shoulder a minute, he knew that she was still in pain, and yet his "special" back took center stage again. She shook her head no.

"What do you mean?" he asked.

"I'm not going to hurt my shoulder any more than it already is," she said in a firm voice, surprising herself more than him.

"But I'm stressed out," he said, as if he couldn't understand why his concerns wouldn't override her pain.

"So am I," she said, then went into the kitchen for a drink of water.

He followed her into the kitchen. "What do you have to be stressed about?" he asked, sounding truly perplexed. "I'm doing the hard stuff at work."

She felt instantaneously enraged. Then she bit her lip knowing that if she didn't come up with the right response he'd probably turn it around on her and say something like, "After all I've done for you. . . ." So she decided to give him a paradoxical compliment. She said, "You seem to deal with stress better than I do."

"Well, I do have more of it. . . ." he began.

"And you can go without a back rub while I can't."

"Oh," he said, sounding proud of himself, then seeming befuddled.

She rubbed her shoulder, trying to look receptive to the possibility of him resuming his abbreviated back rub. To her surprise, he did begin to rub her shoulder again. Within a few minutes he began trying to seduce her. She responded by saying, "What about my back rub?"

"But this will help release tension, too," he said.

"Maybe for you now, but as I said, you deal with stress better than me. A back rub would be great."

He gave her the back rub that she requested. Afterward, Barbara went to sleep. Each evening after work for the next week, she made sure that if he asked for a back rub she received one too. By the end of the week he started complaining about being too tired to reciprocate. So she began to insist on receiving hers first. She used the rationale that she would be more relaxed to give him the kind of back rub that he deserved.

The Next Obstacle

Next she shifted her attention to his complaints about coworkers and how much he had done for them. It was clear to her that she couldn't just bluntly bring it up; she had to sit back and wait. Bryan didn't keep her waiting long. During dinner he said in a sour voice, "Do you know what Jim asked me today?"

She knew that in the past when she'd simply ask, "What?" he would lay out his complaints, so this time she made a nurturing comment with a paradoxical twist. "I don't know, but he sure does talk about how generous you are with advice."

He choked on the water he was sipping.

"Are you okay?" she asked.

He nodded. "Did he really say that?"

"Sure did. Everyone appreciates how knowledgeable you are. And they think you never complain about sharing that knowledge."

"Well, I don't," he said unconvincingly.

"I know, honey," she said with a smile. "How about a back rub? I've had a hard day."

Had Barbara continued to give Magnificent Mike what he wanted it would have been a losing arrangement not only for her but for him, too. Letting him be the "special" partner would have deprived him of the benefit of a balanced relationship. If his own needs were all he knew, he would sink into a deep emotional freeze. She began to give him the opportunity to thaw and to enjoy being enriched by knowing her. Reciprocity makes a healthy relationship. And Magnificent Mike sours your relationship by trying to turn you into his slave or admirer.

KEEPING THE CODE

With a Magnificent Mike, you need to strive for a relationship based on CODE concepts. To achieve **C**ompassion, **O**penness,

Depth, and Equality in a relationship with this type of spoiled man, you should:

- Expect him to acknowledge you as someone unique and special, just as he is.
- Expect him to take care of you as you take care of him.
- Expect him to give you time equal to the time you give him.

If you're married to a Magnificent Mike, he probably won't admit that there is no reciprocity in your relationship. When you complain that there isn't, he'll tell you that you're wrong. In fact, he probably takes this tactic one step further by telling you that it's really you who doesn't give enough. It can be difficult for him to acknowledge being wrong, so he tries to make you feel bad about it even though he's actually the one who's at fault. This tactic keeps you off-balance and always wondering if you are wrong and he is right.

Magnificent Mike dumps his disturbing emotions on others. If he's angry at someone and finds it hard to resolve those feelings, he'll dump them on you. Those emotions are like hot potatoes that he'll toss to you as soon as they come up for him; this way he doesn't have to resolve the emotions himself. One classic example of this tactic is to get angry at you when he is actually angry at something else. You may wonder why on earth he would punish you instead of the person or even the thing that really made him angry. The answer is simple: it's easier to dump it on you than to responsibly face what is really bothering him.

Perhaps you've walked in on him just as he's hanging up the phone and you make the mistake of asking him a simple question. Then he gives you an angry glare.

"Why are you so angry with me?" you ask.

"It's that plumber," he answers, shaking his head. "I hate having to deal with incompetent people!"

Two hours later he gives you another angry glare.

"Now what's the matter?" you ask.

"I'm just angry. Can't you see that?"

It's time for a nurturing comment. Say something like, "Oh yes, I can see that you're angry. He really has got you, hasn't he?" Here you challenge his special sense of power.

"Got me? What are you talking about? That jerk can't get me!"

Now it's time for a paradoxical compliment. Say something like, "I guess you're right. You're too mature to get worked up over him. Sorry, I guess I was mistaken."

"Apology accepted."

He's now in a bind. If he complains about that person again, he calls himself a liar and a hypocrite because he's still plugged into the conflict with him.

> BECAUSE HE'S CENTER of the universe, he thinks it's okay to spew out his emotions. He thinks he has the perfect right to vent, and doesn't care if his anger lands on you. He doesn't feel it is inappropriate; to him, nothing he does is inappropriate.

DEGREES OF MAGNIFICENCE

Some Magnificent Mikes are so obvious about their need to get you to focus on them that they get upset if the focus is on you even for the best of reasons. For example, normally you would expect even a casual friend to be pleased when you've accomplished a major feat or have been awarded an honor. But he may appear disappointed, offended, jealous, or even angry. If so, what you assumed to be an intimate relationship may be a one-way street in his direction.

Then there are the Magnificent Mikes who are not so obvious. They can be good at pretending that they are compassionate and generous. Though they express interest in the details of your life, the depth of their interest may not be deeper than what is conventionally expected. Compassion may not be in their emotional vocabulary.

TAKE THESE STEPS

1. Acknowledge his specialness by noting that you both have unique talents.
2. Ask him to take care of you when you are in need just as you take care of him in the same kind of circumstances.
3. Take away the time you give him when he does not reciprocate by giving you his time.
4. Let him know your plan to take further time for yourself even after he gets upset about it.

> YOU MAY FEEL as if his competitiveness is a call for you to let him win when he competes with you. Don't let him win and don't even bother to compete. That probably sounds contradictory. The point is, it's healthier for you (and him, too) for you not to get dragged down to his level.

If you find that he expresses concern or compassion that is not consistent with what you have experienced from him in the past and you judge it as insincere, don't reject it out of hand. Use this expression as an opportunity to break new ground. It's important to let him know that his showing compassion toward you isn't consistent with how he's been treating you, but tell him tactfully. He'll use it against you if you tell him directly and try to make you feel ungrateful.

He may say "You're acting surprised that I'm concerned." Or "How can you imply that I'm not concerned? Why even try with you?"

Don't take the bait and answer directly. Say something like "It feels good to hear you say that you're concerned."

He may persist as a way for him to turn your gain into his. He'll probably say something like "I'm concerned about you."

At this point, you can subtly imply that he is wrong by saying, "Oh, that's nice to hear. Thanks."

MAKING YOUR RELATIONSHIP A TWO-WAY STREET

Here is an example of how it is possible to turn a Magnificent Mike's behavior around by being overly sympathetic to the point where he realizes how foolish he sounds. Say, for example, your mother just died. He would probably know that the obvious social expectation requires that he make a statement of condolence such as "Oh, I'm sorry about your mother." Then he may manipulate your grief by saying, "I'm still trying to get over the loss of my mom, too."

"Oh, I'm sorry," you counter.

"You know that she was a jewel, always there for me," he says. "I've never been able to find anyone who is as compassionate and caring."

"That's the way I feel . . ." you begin.

He hangs his head despondently, distracting you from what you were feeling about your own mother. Now it's his grief that captures your attention. Then he says, "She was one of those people who really put herself out there for me."

"Just like my mother," you begin again.

"But my mother really went the extra mile. Remember the time when she . . ."

He not only cut you off from your grief about the loss of your mother, but he added that his mother was more special than yours. He also managed to slip in another insidious message. This one is designed to put you on notice that you too are being evaluated for your worth to him. Since he said that his mother went the extra mile for him, he challenged you to prove that you could too. He accomplished all this while pretending to give you empathetic condolences.

What could've been an opportunity to receive emotional support from him turned into the opposite. He manipulated your grief to praise himself and his mother for having the exceptional selflessness to take care of him.

Use a nurturing comment to turn his one-way street into a two-way street. Say something like, "I can understand that it was a terrible loss for you. She really knew how to cherish you."

"Yeah, uh . . ." he begins.

"Maybe we can have a portion of my mom's funeral devoted to your mom. After all, they were friends."

"Are you kidding? That's not right, it's her time."

"Do you mean that?"

"Yeah. And you, too. It must be hard for you."

"Good point. Thanks."

Magnificent Mike needs to learn that his "special needs" are all in his mind. It's best to trap him into revealing it to himself. This way you won't be accused of hurting his "special feelings." Remember to:

- Take the logical extension of his demands for special attention to its ridiculous extreme.
- Acknowledge his opinion of himself but don't give him the impression that you agree with it.
- Hold back favors if he doesn't offer anything in return.

MAUREEN AND PHIL

Life was going well for Maureen and Phil for the first few months of their relationship. At least that was what Maureen thought. She believed she had never met anyone as talented and accomplished until she saw his apartment when they came home from a weekend in Tahoe.

His refrigerator looked like a giant science experiment. "I shouldn't have let my friend Darren stay here while we were away."

Maureen took another look at the jars of ancient mayonnaise and mustard, and containers of half-eaten food. The mold obviously predated the weekend. In fact, all of it looked like it predated their relationship.

"Has Darren been living here since last year?" She laughed hoping that he'd join her.

Phil shook his head. "Why?"

She laughed again playfully, trying to get him to join in. "This stuff looks like an archaeologist could date it."

"Are you saying I'm a liar?" he asked with bitter indignity.

First Red Flags

Maureen took a deep breath and stepped back. *Where did that come from?* she wondered. Was this the same guy who had so impressed her over the past few months?

She walked into the cluttered living room. Cleaning off a space to sit took a few minutes. A dog-eared copy of Machiavelli's *The Prince* lay on top of the stack of debris on the coffee table.

"Is this your book?" she asked.

"Are you critical of that, too?"

"I didn't say that. I'm sorry."

"Good. Now let's get back to the reason why we came here," he said as he sat down and put her arms around her.

It was hard for her to warm up to him after those strange interactions. She managed to excuse herself by saying that she needed to drop by her mother's house. Despite his protest that she was leaving, she knew that she needed to be the one to decide when she would leave, not him. Yet he persisted, only to make her feel even more uncomfortable. When she returned home she found an angry message waiting for her on her answering machine.

She decided to come in for counseling because she was unsure about what direction to take in the relationship. Within the first few minutes she described seeing the book *The Prince*. I told her that it was known to be a treatise on reaching your goals no matter what the costs. It was summed up in the phrase: The end justifies the means. Within the context of the relationship this all seemed to imply that his goals were to do whatever he could do to convince her that he was an ideal mate—at least until she upset his efforts by deciding to leave when she wanted to, not when he wanted her to.

Plan of Action

In our session we also talked about how she should make it clear to him that she would not put up with his narcissism. The tricky part was to do it in a way that used the context of the situation to make the point.

The next day she arrived for a lunch date at a restaurant downtown and just around the corner from the mortgage broker's office where he worked. She looked around for him but, seeing he wasn't there, picked a table and told the waitress that she would be expecting a friend.

Two men in suits talked animatedly at the next table. It was hard not to eavesdrop because their gossip was so engrossing. They talked about a colleague who was super-competitive and who would stop at nothing to get to the top.

She was so absorbed in their story that when Phil walked into the restaurant she was disappointed.

"And speak of Machiavelli now," said one of the men.

She gasped as they stood up to greet him.

"Hey guys!" Phil said. "You want to join me and my girl-friend over here?"

They graciously introduced themselves to Maureen but they said they were just on their way out.

"People you work with?" she asked.

"Yeah. They serve their purpose," he said and picked up the menu.

Responding to Red Flags

She wanted to ask him what purpose *she* served to him but let that thought pass. She decided that if their relationship had any chance of going anywhere that she wanted it to go, she would need to respond to the red flags and work around his defensiveness.

Focusing directly on him or their relationship would spike his defensiveness. The departure of his colleagues presented an opportunity. "So what purpose do they serve?"

He looked at her suspiciously for a few moments. Finally he said, "I've got them helping with a report for the CEO. When I get a promotion they'll want to move up with me. They're in it for themselves."

She noticed how quickly he moved to distrust their intentions when the original question was what purpose they served for him. He managed to keep the focus off of himself, while accusing them of using him. In group therapy she had learned about projection. This is a defense mechanism that involves projecting onto another person what you actually believe or feel.

"Must be hard thinking that people are using you."

He nodded yes. The waitress arrived and he ordered for both of them.

"Maybe they feel as badly about being used as you do," she suggested.

He looked stunned as he struggled with how to answer that question. She had found a seam in his tightly woven defensive system. She had also put him on notice without saying that she too didn't want to be taken for granted as another person who served a purpose.

"By the way, I didn't want a pastrami sandwich," she said, waving down the waiter. She reordered.

"It's a good sandwich," he said as if she had insulted his taste.

"I hope you enjoy yours. But I don't eat red meat. Didn't I tell you?" she said, knowing quite well that she had already told him—twice, in fact.

He shrugged his shoulders. "Anyway, I need to get my apartment back in shape. Do you think you'd be willing to help?"

"You wouldn't want me to feel used like you or your coworkers, would you?"

"Of course not!" he said emphatically. "What do you take me for?"

"I'm hoping you're somebody who doesn't want to put me in a position like that ever again."

This story illustrates that despite the fact that Maureen confronted Phil only twice, she was able to break ground in her effort to make it clear that she offered only a balanced relationship.

SUMMING UP MAGNIFICENT MIKE

Mike gets you to spoil him by making you think he is better than you are. He acts as though he has special talents and needs to conserve his energy for those talents. He needs you to praise his talents and feels wounded if you don't.

Your plan should be to get balance back in your relationship. You should expect to be taken care of just as he expects you to take care of him. Allow him special favors if, and only if, he genuinely reciprocates. You should strive for mutual magnificence—both of you need to be recognized for having special talents.

CHAPTER 12

checkup quiz
Humbling Magnificent Mike

1. When he asks you to take care of him because he needs to rest up to preserve his talents:
   a. Comply with his wishes because if you don't the world won't benefit from his special talents.
   b. Allow him to show you how special he is by allowing you to rest up, too.
   c. Tell him that he's not so special if he needs you to help him rest.
   d. Soothe him and praise him for his special talents.

2. If he tells you how much he has taught you and that you need to pay him back:
   a. Thank him profusely for being such a great mentor.
   b. Pay him back by deferring your own needs.
   c. Feel grateful and inadequate.
   d. Ask him why you would need to repay him.

3. When he asks for special favors and grants you none:
   a. Be patient—he'll get around to it.
   b. Make the special favors not so special.
   c. Stop giving him special favors.
   d. Assume that he needs those special favors.

4. When he argues that his job is much more stressful than yours:
   a. Believe him because he knows best.
   b. Acknowledge that he feels that his job is stressful and ask him not to second-guess yours.
   c. Go to his workplace to verify that.
   d. Do your best to help cushion his stress.

5. If you both experience a loss and he describes his sense of loss as greater:
   a. Give him more support and forget your grief.
   b. Think of him as being more sensitive.
   c. Do your best to take care of yourself.
   d. Tell him to stop being selfish.

6. If he wants you to give up your job to take better care of him:
   a. Do it because taking care of him is a more important job.
   b. Don't do it and tell him that both of you can take better care of each other.
   c. Tell him to quit his job to take care of you.
   d. Try harder to take care of him while you work.

7. If he uses his anger to keep you from criticizing his sense of specialness:
   a. Keep from saying anything that remotely looks like criticism.
   b. Praise him to high heaven for everything.
   c. Argue with him to get your confidence up.
   d. Communicate clearly, and if he needs to be confronted do so in a neutral voice.

8. When he dictates the schedule for both of you:
   a. Work to a compromise and make it fit your needs as well.
   b. Give in to avoid arguments.
   c. Always be early to events that he has scheduled.
   d. Refuse to be on his schedule.

9. If he tries to get you to obsess with him about petty details about his life:
   a. Tell him that you appreciate how he includes you in his life.
   b. Broaden the conversation and resist his attempt to tie you up in his details.
   c. Ask him thousands of questions about those details.
   d. Listen patiently until he gets tired.

10. When his eyes glaze over or he quickly changes the subject back to himself when you talk about stress that you are experiencing:
    a. Tell him that you don't have the emotional energy to talk to him now.
    b. Go ahead and talk about his concerns because that's the best you'll get from him.
    c. Assume that you're stressing over something not really that stressful.
    d. Cry because you might as well be alone.

13

Transforming Traditional Tom

You remember Traditional Tom. He may hide behind tradition or even a self-serving interpretation of a religious text to get you to wait on him. He'll say he's "old-fashioned" when the truth is that he's stuck in the time warp of sexism and patriarchal control.

You are in a far better position to resist this type of spoiled behavior than your mother or grandmother was because you have modern society on your side. So take advantage of the support that was not available to women of previous generations.

> TOM, OR *Shrink-to-Fit Man*, wants you to fit in with his small, antiquated perspective. However, there is no equality in a relationship where shared rights do not exist or where one person expects the other to conform.

Traditional Toms have the best deal among spoiled men because they don't have to rely solely on themselves to manipulate you into spoiling them. They can also rely on friends, family, and their community.

One of the most common ways a Traditional Tom gets you

to spoil him is by making you to do all the housework. Over fifty years ago, the principal breadwinner was usually the husband, and most women (who did not work outside the home) were referred to as "homemakers." Now, however, dual-income families are very common, and even if the woman doesn't work she is not expected to stay at home all day cleaning.

Notice in the following story about Linda and Joseph how Linda managed to gently shift him into sharing the responsibility of the housework.

LINDA AND JOSEPH

After thirty years of marriage, Linda felt worn. She and her husband, Joseph, raised two sons who grew up to be mature and independent young men. But she still felt that there were demands on her that were hard to identify, so she came in for counseling. She said that Joseph often complained about the burden of being the breadwinner along with doing all of the yard work, and the barbecue on Sundays.

Linda started working when the boys were in high school, yet she still ran the household, cooked the meals, cleaned up afterward, and did the rest of the housework. Before the boys left home, Joseph had them doing most of the yard work for him and he managed to do only the occasional barbecue. After the boys left home, he didn't pick up the slack in the yard. It seemed to Linda that his easy chair was getting worn out, just like her.

Confronting Red Flags

The Sunday afternoon after her second counseling session she was trying to vacuum the family room. As usual Joseph sat in his easy chair, watching the second of his two football games. "Honey, please turn that off," Joseph said straining his neck to see the tube as she vacuumed in front of him.

"Would you like me to do it without the electricity?"

"That would be great," he said as he threw up his hands, seeing that the referee pulled a yellow penalty flag on the play.

She looked at him and shook her head. After a big sigh she turned off the vacuum. Yet she continued to push the vacuum around as if it were doing its job. She glanced at him, but he didn't seem to notice what she was doing. "Wow," she said. "The silent mode is more powerful! Thanks for the idea, honey. I'm pulling up all sorts of dirt."

"Good job," he said, with his eyes glued to the tube.

She pushed the vacuum under his legs on his recliner. Again he craned his neck to see the game. Then, as if someone had given him a cold slap in the face, his eyes widened. "What in the hell are you doing?"

"What does it look like?" she answered as she continued to pretend to vacuum.

"Have you seen your doctor recently?"

She shook her head, then took out one of the attachments to vacuum the upholstery on the chair.

"Stop it!" he shouted.

"But honey! I've got work to get done."

"It's done for today," he said with certain finality. "Sit down and watch the game."

She glanced at the game then back at him and decided to test him by saying, "No, I think only men can understand that game."

"I'll explain it," he said, taking her bait.

"Only if you promise to vacuum this room afterward."

"What kind of deal is that?"

"Honey, if I don't clean, the house would be filthy. Of course, if you don't want to teach me about the game. . . ."

"Yeah, uh, sure," he responded, sounding perplexed by what he had gotten himself into.

She sat down on the couch and asked, "So, who is winning?"

Linda's Persistence

Later that afternoon she walked back into the family room and saw that Joseph, her Traditional Tom, hadn't budged an inch. The second game was over and he was watching ESPN for a wrap-up of all the other games.

She pointed to the vacuum.

"Oh, I'll get to it later. Go get the steaks ready for the barbecue."

She bit her tongue to keep from telling him what she really felt. She knew that if she prepared the steaks her advantage of catching him off-balance would be lost. "I think you'll have to prep the steaks while I vacuum in here."

"But you always do the prep. It's our deal. I do the barbecuing."

"You mean you stand over the barbecue and turn the steaks over a few times."

"What's got into you?"

She reflected for a moment, trying to suppress her anger. "Just tired, I guess. Watching the game was the only time I have been able to sit down."

"Sit down more often."

"Sure," she said knowing that appealing to his sense of power would help.

"Good!"

She shrugged her shoulders. "Well, I've got to get this vacuuming done."

"What about the steaks?"

"Oh? Did you really mean it about inviting me to sit with you?"

"Of course I did!"

"Then what would you rather do, the vacuuming or the prep on the steaks?"

He looked befuddled. "I guess the vacuuming."

She gave him a kiss then went into the kitchen to begin to

prep the steaks. By the time she took out the knife and the cutting board he had turned off the vacuum. She put the knife down and walked into the family room.

"Steaks ready?" he asked gleefully.

"I haven't even started and it looks like you haven't either."

"What do you mean? I vacuumed the best I could."

She stared back at him with a blank face.

"I might as well not even try," he said with a sour tone, looking away.

At this point, she knew that she had to resist taking his bait and allowing him to play victim. In the past she would help him make excuses by saying, "Oh, no, you did a good job, honey." No! Not this time, she thought. She had to make clear that his effort was minimal while tricking him into trying harder.

She smiled sympathetically. "It's a good start, honey. I guess we have to decide together who should finish the job."

"If you want it done any better, do it after dinner," he said matter-of-factly.

"Yes, but there's a lot to clean up after dinner."

"Why are you making such a big deal out of this?"

Linda picked up the vacuum wand and said, "I guess you're right. Let's just do our jobs and have dinner."

She turned on the vacuum and he skulked into the kitchen and did his own prep work with the steaks.

Joseph grumped his way through dinner.

She did her best to not ask what was wrong. She knew that she would get a lecture on a women's role. "Honey, these steaks are great," she said.

He gave her a nasty look.

She smiled. "All great cooks are excellent at prep."

"They are?" he asked.

She took another bite and nodded with certainty.

Just like Linda, you too can help yourself by not responding to his bait to get you to spoil him. Turn the tables on him without overtly resisting his demands. Unfortunately, there is no quick fix with a Traditional Tom. It took Linda many months to change the dynamics in her relationship by persistence and consistency. When you make similar changes, ask for support from those who don't buy his traditional model so that you feel more hopeful and less isolated.

You too can make changes in your relationship to a Traditional Tom. Keep focused on your plan and follow constructive steps.

TAKE THESE STEPS

1. Let him know that you have your feet firmly planted in the twenty-first century and that you expect mutual respect and nurturance despite the traditions of the past.
2. Establish a support system, even if it's outside of the family, church, or your mutual friends, for when he tries to rally the troops to isolate you.
3. Say that you have a different interpretation of scripture if he tries to claim that you are not pious based on scripture.
4. Stay consistent despite his tactics when he tells you that you're acting like a "crazy feminist" or are from the "Left Coast."

If your mother and grandmother lived in a society where they were second-class citizens within their marriage, it doesn't mean that you have to live that way, too. You may hope that he will understand and treat you differently, but waiting and hoping for him to understand won't make it happen unless you change your expectations.

Just like other spoiled men, he's not going to like your new expectations. He'll probably complain that you're moving into taboo territory. Consider his complaints simply as barks. Old dogs can learn new tricks. He may bark many times before getting the idea that you mean business.

Let him get uncomfortable. Expect it. Then stay firm in your expectation that his privileged position needs to change. He can hold onto his privileges if you get privileges to match. Dealing with some Traditional Toms this way will tip the scales to even. You simply ask for equal time, saying that "it's only fair." But for most women this is only the first step.

You can outsmart a Traditional Tom. Remember to:

- Put him in a bind so that his requests conflict with each other.
- Use his beliefs to turn the tables on him.
- Snap him out of his time warp by challenging the past with the present.

IMPORTANCE OF A SUPPORT SYSTEM

A Traditional Tom probably has friends or family who back his belief that he's entitled to be waited on. They may or may not know the extreme that he's taken those beliefs to get you to spoil him. Either way, it's always helpful to get support.

If you don't look for support outside of his supporters in the traditionalist circle, Traditional Tom can make you feel hopeless by trying to convince you there is nowhere to turn. If you do try to seek support from people outside your usual group and feel you are hemmed in on all sides it can seem like a no-win situation. The situation is not hopeless and you need not feel powerless.

I want to acknowledge your discomfort in stepping out of your reference group. Not only are you trapped in a subservient role to him, but you've got the people around you weighing you down with their agreement of how "it's got to be." Your

friends might say, "Buck up, girl! That's just the way things are."
It's an understatement that your Traditional Tom isn't going to
like it if you try to change things. He'll rally the troops against
you, and that may include friends and family who believe their
faith or tradition dictates what a woman's position in marriage
should be.

RELIGIOUS IMPLICATIONS

Studies have shown that the majority of people believe in a God
of some type. The key is that increasing numbers of deeply
pious people also believe in equality between the sexes. The
tide is shifting. Don't wait until Traditional Tom catches on; he
is counting on you to not notice.

The point is: don't let him use religion against you. Throughout history many societies have claimed to have greater piety
than all others. Some even raped and pillaged while claiming
to have God on their side. Though the things they did to the
victims were evil, they claimed that, according to God, the victims were the evil ones.

Let me make this perfectly clear. I am not suggesting that
you go against God. Your reverence for God does not have to
be dictated by your husband or partner's frame of reference.
I can't believe that God wants you to be subservient to your
husband or partner. You shouldn't, either.

THE USE OF PIETY

Traditional Tom can claim to be more pious than you are, especially if he can use that piety to get you to spoil him. He's got
to convince you that God wants you to spoil him. Of course, he
doesn't use the term *spoil*; he wants you to revere him. Unfor-

tunately, the type of reverence he offers in return doesn't equal the type of reverence he wants from you. He can't do this without you believing that this arrangement is sanctified by God.

If he or perhaps both of you are part of a religious group that adheres to a fundamentalist interpretation of the Bible, the Koran, or other religious text, you may feel that your subservient role is sanctified by God or another "higher power." Did you notice that I used the word *interpretation*? Rather than get involved in a theological debate, let's agree that there are many pious people who hold to different interpretations of their religious texts.

A Traditional Tom has a personal stake in maintaining his traditional top-dog position. How wonderfully convenient for him to be able to refer to "God's will" as a way to keep you spoiling him. This puts you in a no-win situation, because if you resist his efforts you may think you are going against God. Consider the case of Terri and Aaron and how she worked hard to find support to go from feeling powerless to feeling hopeful.

TERRI AND AARON

Piety was something that both Terri and Aaron strove for in their relationship. They wanted to keep their lives and their marriage in sync with God's plan for them.

Interpreting what that plan was, however, seemed to be a little difficult. On the way home from church every Sunday, Aaron offered his commentary to the sermon given by the minister. On each ride home, Terri felt incredibly tense as she tried to see the connection between what Aaron was saying and the minister's sermon. He seemed to slant the minister's words to support a favored position of men over women.

Terri wanted to say that she didn't agree, but she believed that it wasn't her place to say anything. Yet she resented not feeling justified to express a different opinion. She simply felt powerless. After Aaron finished his commentary he would ask for her opinion, which really was a request for her to say that she agreed with him.

Terri's TRAPped Feelings

His tactics made her feel TRAPped every Sunday. Far from being a pious day, Sunday became a day she dreaded. Finally, she told herself, "He's not taking Sunday away from me." She liked going to church and she always enjoyed the minister's sermon.

She had heard that the minister had recently earned a master's degree in counseling. That got her thinking that she could ask him for some advice. She knew that she had nothing to lose, because if he agreed with Aaron's point of view she would only feel as TRAPped as before.

She called the minister for an appointment during the middle of the week when Aaron was working. He agreed to meet her the next day.

"You and Aaron aren't having marital problems, are you?" he asked.

This opening question worried her. She assumed that he would take Aaron's side. "I'm not here to say anything disrespectful about my husband. Or challenge a man's authority."

"Authority? It's only God that has authority."

"But Aaron serves the path of God. Isn't that authority?"

"So do you, sister. Where did you get the idea that he has any more authority than you?"

She stared back at him, wondering if she was really hearing him say that. Perhaps there was a parable somewhere in his words. "He said that man's authority over women was the message of your sermons."

"My sermons?" the minister asked, looking uncomfortable with the implications.

"I love him. He's a good man. But he's got me believing that you support that message."

"God wants you to serve each other," he said sympathetically.

She started weeping in relief, prompting him to comfort her. "If you want to bring him for pastoral counseling, I'm available at any time."

She hugged him, then rushed out to tell Aaron.

Aaron's Persistence with Tradition

"What on earth did you tell him?" Aaron shouted.

"Nothing," she said.

"Don't you realize what you did to me?!"

She was horrified at what she must have done. Perhaps he thought his standing in the church was ruined. As she tried to gather herself she remembered that the minister had invited her to come back with him. "He wants us to come in."

"Are you serious? So I can get scolded in front of my wife? No way!"

"But he said that he could help," she pleaded.

"Help with what? I've got to go in there myself and clear things up," he said, then retreated to the den.

Aaron's brother and sister-in-law both gave her the cold shoulder at church the next Sunday.

She didn't know where to turn. Apparent isolation and the family opinion against her made everything look bleak.

Terri's Like-Minded Support System

One day, Rebecca, a casual acquaintance from Bible study, waved her over to the church entrance and invited her to go on morning walks with her. But she had always kept her distance from Rebecca because Aaron had called her "a woman moving out of the flock." When she asked him for clarification, he told her that Rebecca demanded a lot from her husband.

"I'll meet you at the town square tomorrow about nine."

Rebecca smiled. It looked to Terri as if she was relieved that someone in the church still considered her a friend.

The walk that morning started with Terri feeling terribly guilty, as if she was doing something criminal. But as she began to enjoy the morning air, she shed that guilt. She knew that she needed to talk to someone. The minister had opened the door to hope. Yet Aaron had quickly slammed it shut.

"Could we walk in a less prominent area of town?" Terri asked.

"You're worried that people would know that we're friends."

"No. No, I just don't want it to get back to Aaron. Then he'll blame what I did on your influence."

"Wow. What did you do?"

"I went to talk to the minister about our marriage," Terri said, as if she had disclosed a deep dark secret.

"Good God! I thought you were going to tell me that you had an affair or something," Rebecca laughed. "I went to see him, too. Then I brought Hayden."

"Did he get outraged, too?"

"Well, he's doing the dishes now," Rebecca laughed.

"That's why some of the men say that you strayed from the flock?" she asked as she reflected on how powerful the shunning had been and for so trivial an offense.

"I forgave them and moved on," she said with a sigh. "Now you go talk to the minister again."

Terri did go back to the minister and she was completely relieved to find out that the bridges weren't burnt. Quite to the contrary, he was a great support.

He helped her plan to do a lot of little things at once to change her relationship so that Aaron would feel the tidal shift and not be able to put his finger on any one change in her behavior.

Now on the drive home from church on Sundays she changed the subject when he brought up the sermon. Eventually, she told him that she didn't agree with his critique of the sermon. Then he changed the subject.

Terri's Consistency Against Spoiling

One evening when returning from church Aaron asked Terri to bring him some snacks. She replied that her hands were dirty from cleaning the floor and perhaps he could either get them himself or clean the rest of the floor while she prepared snacks.

"I don't ask you to mow the lawn, do I?"

She reflected for a moment. This was an opportunity. "I'd love to switch jobs with you."

"What's got into you? You don't know the first thing about mowers and I don't know about housework. Let's keep it that way."

"I'd rather learn to appreciate what you do by trying it out," she said, careful not to actually say that she wanted him to appreciate what she did. She wanted that implied.

"If you want to mow today, that would be good," he said with a laugh. "I'd rather watch the game."

"Sure," she said. "I'll do that after the floor. Then you can put together some dinner after your game."

"Wait. . . ." he began.

But she was already back in the kitchen. She finished up quickly, then went out to mow the lawn. That went so fast that she started weeding to finish off the afternoon.

When she walked into the house at 6:00, he was fast asleep in his chair. He woke up, startled by the screen door slamming shut. "What's for dinner?"

"That's your decision, chef. I'm going to take a shower."

"But I . . ." he began, but once again she was in the next room by the time he finished whatever he was trying to say.

She returned an hour later. He still hadn't moved from his chair. "Could you whip something up?"

She was on a roll and she didn't want him to slam on the brakes. "That wasn't our deal," she said.

"I didn't agree to that."

"Then you should have told me before I did all that yard work. In fact, I liked the yard work so much let's call Sunday, your *chef's day*."

She waited another hour before he grew so frustrated and hungry that he stomped into the kitchen. "I have no idea what to make."

"Whatever you want, honey."

He finally put together cheese sandwiches. They were terrible but she acted like they were superb. "Good job, chef!"

The next Sunday she made sure to get out to the lawn early before he could object. She waited for him to put together some semblance of dinner and received it with compliments and gratitude.

This was the crack in the wall that she had hoped for. Over the next few months she would exploit similar cracks. Eventually she began to feel that she was cultivating a marriage based on mutual respect.

With a traditional man it will take a lot of work and admittedly some very uncomfortable moments to convince him of a change in roles. Stay consistent with your tactics to stimulate change. Keep in mind the relationship CODE and strive for the compassion, openness, depth, and equality that will bring about a marriage or relationship that is a true partnership.

CHANGE THROUGH ONE CONVERSATION

In the following story of Carlos and Judy's marriage, notice how it only takes one conversation to begin resisting the traditional role that he is trying to force her into.

Carlos comes home each night from work expecting a good hot meal. She works too, but she doesn't get to plop down in front of the tube to unwind like he does.

One night after dinner she glanced over to the family room where he sat on the recliner. She asked him to help with the dishes.

"Oh, come on, honey. You know I've had a hard day at work."

"Don't you think I had a hard day too?"

Carlos hit the mute button on the television remote and said, "Sure, I know it's been hard for you. But it's not the same thing."

She noticed that it was halftime on the football game. "Are you saying I don't have a man's job?"

"Well, yeah," he said as he glanced back at the television, noticing that the game had resumed. "After you finish up, join me over here."

She knew that he didn't mean for her to take a break; he meant for her to bring him a tray of snacks. The prospect of repeating this scene endlessly in the future grated on her. She left the dishes on the table and walked into the family room. Then she stood staring at him as he watched the game. She decided to escape from the bind that he put her in by pretending to give up. "I can't handle my job and take care of the house at the same time," she said.

"That's nice, honey," he said wincing at a botched play in the game.

"Okay, I'll quit my job," she said in a matter-of-fact tone.

Carlos sighed and pressed the mute button on the remote. "Honey, we need the money, you know that the payments on my . . . our new truck . . ."

"Yes, but you deserve to be taken care of better. I think I'll put in my resignation tomorrow."

"You're doing fine. Just get the tray and join me."

"Sorry, I can't even finish the dishes. You do them. I'm going to bed."

The point of this vignette is to show that even in one conversation you can call his attention to the fact that a shift in your status needs to be made. And you can do this by outsmarting him little by little and convincing him that you're not in the wrong.

> MANY SPOILED MEN believe you should be subservient to them. What do *you* believe? You should know that you are his equal and you deserve to be treated the way he expects you to treat him. Work toward and insist upon nothing less than that ideal. If he doesn't agree, find someone else who will treat you with the respect you deserve.

SUMMING UP TRADITIONAL TOM

Traditional Tom refers to tradition to get you to spoil him. He recruits friends and family who belong to your subculture to support his favored position. If you go against him and his supporters, you risk isolation. He may even use religious texts to support his favored position.

Your plan should be to keep your focus on the twenty-first century and resist his efforts to roll back the clock. When he recruits others stuck in the past, form alliances with people who have their feet firmly planted in the twenty-first century with you. If he uses a religious text to support him, tell him that you have a different interpretation. Invite him to join you in mutual respect and nurturance.

To move your relationship into the realm of equal rights and respect, you must tell him that:

- You expect mutual respect and caring.
- You expect a partnership.
- Your interpretation of a woman's role is different than his and is valid.

CHAPTER 13

checkup quiz
Transforming Traditional Tom

1. When he goes into the den and sits on the couch after dinner and asks you to bring dessert:
   a. Say, "Sure honey."
   b. Say, "I'll be glad to do that after you help with the dishes."
   c. Feel taken for granted in silence.
   d. Bake him a fresh pie and make sure it's delicious.

2. When he tells you that God wants you to serve him:
   a. Tell him that you'll do your best to be pious.
   b. Ask him to join you in a twenty-first century version of piety and serve each other.
   c. Say "Amen" and bow to him.
   d. Tell him that he is a sanctimonious bore.

3. When he tells you that you don't understand because he is from Mars and you are from Venus and that he needs to go to his cave:
   a. Help him make the den his cave sanctuary.
   b. Tell him that you don't share his silly rationalization.
   c. Study Martians and learn about his needs.
   d. Keep out of his cave!

4. If he drums up support for his privileged position with friends and family members:
   a. Assume that you are surrounded and there's no use fighting back.
   b. Develop a support system even if it means going outside the family and your old friends.
   c. Argue with them all.
   d. Learn how the other women serve their men.

5. If he tells you that you're going against tradition by not serving him:
   a. Get clear on the tradition.
   b. Tell him that you're updating traditions.
   c. Believe that you can't go against the sea of history.
   d. Tell him that you hate tradition.

6. If he asks you to serve him and his friends every Monday night for the football game but doesn't reciprocate for you on another night:
   a. Figure that boys will be boys.
   b. Make each Monday unpleasant.
   c. Go out with friends on Monday night.
   d. Make Monday rival Sunday as a sacred day because he worships football.

7. If he tells you that you are "out of the norm" and from the "Left Coast":
   a. Tell him you are sorry and you will make it up to him.
   b. Say "Thanks—I'm hoping you'll join me."
   c. Realign yourself with his expectations.
   d. Tell him that he's a right-wing bigot.

8. If he tells you that the inside of the house is your responsibility to maintain:
   a. Do a good job in the inside of the house.
   b. Hire a housekeeper to check up on your work.
   c. Tell him that you want to share the outside so he can help you inside.
   d. Admire his sense of business.

9. When he tells you that you're not being a good wife:
   a. Try to be a better wife.
   b. Ask him to define a good wife based on what's healthy for both of you.
   c. Feel guilty and substandard.
   d. Tell him that he's not being a good husband.

10. When he tells you that you don't have a job as hard as his:
    a. Give him extra care for working harder.
    b. Tell him he apparently doesn't have a grasp of the demands of your job.
    c. Tell him he's a sexist.
    d. Work harder to make up the difference.

Conclusion

A spoiled man has a knack for drawing the worst out of you. While this is an agonizing experience, it's also an opportunity to take a deeper look at yourself. This self-evaluation can be the fuel for growing as a person and improving your relationship.

You may have unique vulnerabilities to spoiled behavior. There are several possible ways that you may have learned to spoil a man. You may have learned by watching your mother spoil your father or you may have experienced an unfortunate past involving abuse. Or perhaps you began to spoil him because you believe that a bad relationship is better than no relationship at all. Whatever the reason the result is the same: You learned to take care of someone who doesn't need your care in place of taking care of yourself.

If you can't take care of yourself, how you can expect him to take care of you? If you compromise your integrity, you compromise the relationship. Also, if you ask him to nurture you but you won't nurture yourself, he won't do what you ask; he'll treat you the way you treat yourself.

Your plan should be to learn how to take care of yourself to stay balanced while in your relationship. Transform your vulnerabilities into sensitivities. Develop independence so that you can base your relationship on mutual interdependence.

Finally, a word about healthy giving: Nowhere in this book did I advise you to be selfish. Giving without the expectation of receiving anything in return is true giving. Yet giving to a person who only takes contributes to an unhealthy relationship. Strive for a balanced healthy relationship. You deserve no less.

Answer Key for Checkup Questions

Chapter 2: Unspoiling with the CODE

1. b
2. a
3. b
4. c
5. a
6. a
7. b
8. c
9. b
10. b

Chapter 3: Seeing Red Flags

1. d
2. b
3. c
4. a
5. c
6. b
7. b
8. c
9. b
10. c

Chapter 4: Challenging the Victim

1. b
2. c
3. b
4. b
5. b
6. c
7. c
8. b
9. c
10. c

Chapter 5: Sheltering from the Emotional Storm

1. d
2. c
3. a
4. d
5. a
6. c
7. d
8. d
9. c
10. c

Chapter 6: Remaining Optimistic with a Pessimist

1. b
2. a
3. b
4. b
5. b
6. b
7. d
8. c
9. b
10. d

Chapter 7: Walking above Eggshells

1. c
2. b
3. c
4. d
5. d
6. a
7. c
8. c
9. b
10. c

Chapter 8: Detaching Sympathy from the Hypochondriac

1. c
2. d
3. c
4. d
5. b
6. b
7. b
8. b
9. b
10. a

Chapter 9: Avoiding Destructive Arguments

1. b
2. c
3. a
4. b
5. b
6. b
7. b
8. d
9. b
10. b

Chapter 10: Asking More from Passive Pete

1. c
2. d
3. b
4. b
5. a
6. b
7. b
8. a
9. b
10. b

Chapter 11: Holding Slippery Sam Accountable

1. b
2. c
3. c
4. c
5. b
6. c
7. b
8. b
9. c
10. c

Chapter 12: Humbling Magnificent Mike

1. b
2. d
3. c
4. b
5. c
6. b
7. d
8. a
9. b
10. a

Chapter 13: Transforming Traditional Tom

1. b
2. b
3. b
4. b
5. b
6. c
7. b
8. c
9. b
10. b

INDEX

ABOUT THE AUTHORS

John B. Arden, Ph.D., is a psychologist with thirty years of counseling experience, twenty of those years in counseling couples. He is the director of training for mental health for the Kaiser Permanente Medical Centers in Northern California, overseeing the largest mental-health training program in the nation. He has taught in colleges, professional schools, and universities. As the author of five previous books, he has been interviewed by *Fortune*, *Real Simple*, *Redbook*, *Cosmopolitan*, CBS Market Watch, the *San Francisco Chronicle*, many nationally syndicated radio programs, and several other media outlets. John's wife, **Victoria Arden, M.A.,** is an arts educator and has worked in the mental health field. They live in Northern California.